The Inn Crowd

The Inn Crowd

Written and photographed by
JACKIE CARADONIO

Foreword by
BOBBI BROWN & STEVEN PLOFKER

Foreword

BY BOBBI BROWN & STEVEN PLOFKER

I've been a makeup artist for nearly forty years and making women feel beautiful and confident is my life's work. Steven, a businessman and developer, has created many buildings in his signature style. But one of the passions we share—other than for our children and grandchildren—is for our thirty-one-room boutique hotel, The George, in our hometown of Montclair, New Jersey. The George, our first creative collaboration as a couple, was an unlikely project and one we never thought we'd do, until, suddenly, we were in the throes of building and decorating it. Now it's one of our greatest joys—and we know the rest of the innkeepers featured in this book probably feel the same way.

When Jackie shared her vision for *The Inn Crowd*, we felt an instant connection to the concept of creating a welcoming space for others because it tapped into something bigger in our lives: the force of constant change and reinvention. Together, we have changed career paths many times and each time, we find new dreams to pursue. We believe it's never too late to shift gears and innovate, or to try something you've never done before—and that is at the heart of The George.

A fearless spirit lives inside each of the people featured in *The Inn Crowd*. These pages bring us together to tell our stories, share our spaces and, most importantly, communicate the delight, comfort, and warmth our guests feel when they experience what we've all built. There are those who dreamed of this life of hospitality for years, while others stumbled upon it, like Steven and I did. We all share the experience of taking exceptional care of people while they're away from home by enveloping them in beautiful spaces that are both unique and extraordinary.

Warmly,
Bobbi & Steven

Introduction

BY JACKIE CARADONIO

I couldn't say exactly when my love affair with hotels began, but even my earliest memories of playing hotel guest—which I'd guess start around the age of seven—are clear. As the daughter of a general manager, I spent holidays in suites, weekends at brunches. Every year on my birthday, my favorite chocolate éclairs would appear at the breakfast table as if by magic, a gift from the hotel's French pastry chef escorted home in my father's briefcase. With each visit, I delighted in every detail of the hotel experience: the fancy little lotions and soaps, never used but squirrelled away and coveted; the ironed white linens stretched over fluffy beds (not to mention the fact that I never had to make said beds). Everything about a hotel seemed to me like an enchanted world of wonders—so much so that, as an adult, I turned the role of guest into a career as a travel photojournalist and magazine editor.

One of the things I always loved most about hotels was the way they allowed me to try on different personas. As a college student studying in Spain, rather than bunk in a hostel like everyone else, I'd convince my friends to pool our money for a room at the Ritz. And though we'd cram four-wide in a single queen-size bed (to the horror of housekeeping, no doubt), I'd swan through the lobby utterly confident. If I didn't belong in those five-star digs, I was convinced I belonged nowhere.

Part of why I love hotels so much is that my relationship with them—like any good relationship—has evolved, and over the years, I began to form a preference for a very specific kind: small, curated places that weren't perfect so much as perfectly imperfect; places that had personality beyond the tangible, beautiful things. I began to collect these little hideaways, much like the sweet-smelling collection of tiny toiletries I once cherished as a child, and eventually came to realize that though utterly unique, they all had one very special feature in common: a visionary owner (or two) who had poured their heart into every corner and every inch of their distinctive place.

I began to think of them as The Inn Crowd, an elite coterie of creatives breathing audacious new life into the classic formula of the warm bed plus hot meal, adding a heap of design savvy, a splash of above-and-beyond hospitality, and spoonful upon spoonful of refined cuisine. They are interior designers, chefs, fashion directors, artists. They're doctors, entrepreneurs, even software engineers—all drawn to the same path by some snowballing force: a desire to build something special, a wish to bring people together, and a chance to give their lives over to their coveted passions.

Always, I found endless wells of inspiration in the impressive creations of The Inn Crowd. I replicated their design ideas and their recipes. I ordered their duvets and pillows. I wanted nothing but dahlias after my stay at The Inn at Kenmore Hall. I bulk-ordered the same herbal tea I sipped at breakfast at The Villa at Saugerties. I tracked down and purchased the black-and-white poncho in the rooms at Eastwind Oliverea Valley within an hour of checking in.

But the most valuable souvenir I brought home from each of these hotels was a deep sense of respect (and, yes, a little bit of envy) for their creators. Because behind their crisp linens and fluffy muffins were always incredible stories of ingenuity and drive, of risk and reward, of a commitment to something more meaningful than what came before. They've given up careers, and often lucrative ones at that, to make something that speaks more deeply to their souls. Even more astounding, rather than keep it all to themselves, they've generously welcomed others—strangers, no less!—into the exquisite little universes they've created.

I felt the world must know them, not just through beautiful photography of their spaces, but through written accounts of their journeys. And so, it is with much gratitude and admiration that I present to you, dear reader, *The Inn Crowd*. Thanks to the ingenuity and talents of these innkeepers, this book is filled with passion and pain, foibles and feats, tough decisions and hard work, and ultimately, above all else, dreams realized. In their stories, I hope you may find as much inspiration as I did, perhaps even some new meaningful path to pursue. And if, by some chance or fate, that path leads to a lovely little inn of your own, please, I insist, call me. I'd love to be your guest.

Tristate

Made

with Love

LOST FOX INN

Litchfield, Connecticut

It was love at first sight. The place and circumstances—a job interview at a Toronto Starbucks—couldn't have been any less primed for romance, and yet when Tim Trojian first saw Eliza Clark, "I immediately had hearts in my eyes," he recalls. Eliza, an author and HGTV showrunner, was interviewing candidates for an editor position. Tim, an executive chef with an easy smile, was in town from Niagara visiting his sister, one of Eliza's interviewees. It wasn't quite a meet-cute—just a perfunctory introduction as Tim picked up his sister post-interview—but it was all he needed to fall hard for the petite woman with the soft voice. "I spent the rest of the week talking about Eliza," he says.

Nothing came of it. Tim went back to Niagara, and his sister went to work for Eliza. Months passed. One day, lamenting a bad date, Eliza—a single mom who had recently seen her daughter off to college—implored her colleagues to set her up. "How about my brother?" Tim's sister responded. "He hasn't stopped talking about you." Though she hadn't exactly been pining for Tim, Eliza hadn't forgotten him either. "I remember thinking he was super handsome and enormously tall," she says.

As if on cue, Tim materialized in Toronto. There was a first date and a second—and then it was time to say goodbye. But the story didn't end there; it didn't even slow down. The following weeks were a whirlwind of long phone calls, daily love letters, and meet-ups in Montreal whenever they could. They had been on just six official dates when Tim quit his job and moved in with Eliza. A year after that, they were married.

Eliza Clark & Tim Trojian

And then, life took over again. Eliza was suddenly on the road for weeks at a time, producing renovation shows while Tim stayed back in Toronto. One night, she came home from a particularly grueling six-week trip to find he had a bonfire going in the backyard. They opened a bottle of wine and stared at the stars, "and I just remember feeling so overwhelmed by how much I missed him," Eliza says. "I thought, let's stop doing this. Let's find a way to really be together."

The way, they decided, was an inn. It made sense: In a previous life, Eliza had run a little bed-and-breakfast outside of Toronto, and Tim's chef experience gave him plenty of hospitality bona fides. But still, it would take years to come to fruition. The couple bought an old lodge in the Catskills, then moved with Eliza's job to New York City, and once again found themselves in the torturous long-distance song and dance as she continued to pull in a paycheck while he oversaw the upstate renovations. Weekends and the Metro-North railway system were the glue that held them together for nearly three years until, finally, she quit her job and they opened the inn.

They called it Foxfire Mountain House, and it was exactly the life they had imagined. She did the beds. He made the coffee. It was simple and perfect. But then it grew. And grew. Until it was more than just the two of them could handle. They hired a staff, "and suddenly we felt like we'd passed over the hands-on bits that we so enjoyed," Eliza says. A handful of years after that first bonfire epiphany, they found themselves once again pining for a passion project that would bring them together.

The way, of course, was another inn—and this time, there'd be no reality TV to produce, no back-and-forth on the train, no division of labor. This time they'd do it like they had envisioned, side by side, hand in hand.

They found it in Litchfield, Connecticut: a trio of buildings—an eighteenth-century tavern and schoolhouse, and a thirty-year-old inn—surrounded by pastoral woodland. It was love at first sight. "Even through the overgrown landscaping and the disrepair, we could see how charming it was and how beautiful it could once again be," Eliza says. In typical fashion, they moved fast. Inspections ensued with no major red flags. Papers were signed and everything looked great—until day one of renovations, when they removed the first piece of drywall. What they found behind virtually every surface? Duct tape. Miles of it holding together shifty electric wiring, even pipes. "It was literally structural duct tape," Tim says, still in disbelief. Elsewhere, they discovered extension cords linked together in dangerous webs that snaked from room to room beneath the floorboards. More extension cords were buried under the grass outside to spread power from inside to outdoor lampposts. In the basement, Tim found the condenser for the air conditioner draining into a mop bucket; a fish tank pump continuously emptied the bucket into a hole that had been drilled into the sewer. It was a series of appalling—not to mention expensive—discoveries.

The budget lurched skyward. The ad hoc piping and electric were excavated, and trenches were dug for new cables and drainage. "You couldn't walk anywhere on the entire property," Eliza recalls. "We laid a literal mile of drainage pipe," Tim adds. Two years would pass before they were finally up to code.

The delay allowed Eliza—along with her daughter, Arden, with whom she now runs the interior design firm Byrd Studio—to fine-tune her design narrative. To bring her vision to life, she created a character, a glamorous and worldly matron personified by this secret wooded inn.

Page 12: A pair of antique portraits believed to be of John and Abigail Adams hangs over the fireplace in the tavern. Eliza retouched the paintings herself.

Previous and above: The tavern's blend of old and new—antique brass ceiling lights, House of Hackney wallpaper—perfectly matches its updated rustic cuisine.

"She knows her wines. She likes finer things," Eliza says. "She has the best linens, the most beautiful art and antiques." Early on, that played out in details like Roman clay applied to the walls and reproductions of crown moldings—all of which Tim worked with local contractors to master.

Central to Eliza's design mission was uniting the property's buildings—a tall order given the nearly three-hundred-year age difference between them. The tavern, built in 1745, and the schoolhouse, constructed in the late eighteenth century and relocated to the property in 1926, retained incredible details—wide chestnut floors, beautifully aged wood paneling, picture windows—that set the perfect tone for her vision. But the circa-1992 inn required more creativity. "Imagine Home Depot in the '90s," Eliza says. "Everything was box, box, box." To soften the hard lines and forge a sense of history, she introduced curves and textures: scalloped light fixtures were hung from the ceilings, New England river stones added dimension to the fireplaces, and in the grand entry, clay brick tile replaced wall-to-wall broadloom carpet.

All the while, Eliza collected vintage pieces in the spirit of her fictional muse. "Antiquing checks all the boxes for me," she says. "It's reusing and repurposing, so you stop something from being thrown away, and you get something truly unique at a really good price." Many a night was spent with a glass (or bottle) of wine as she and Tim scoured resale and antique sites. The next morning, they would set out across the Northeast on pickup missions. In New Jersey, the couple rescued a dozen doors with identical decorative molding; in nearby Greenwich, they scored a round marble-topped table for the tavern; in Maryland, they unearthed a pair of quirky colonial-style portraits, which Eliza retouched herself. Uniting all the spaces across the three buildings, she added more personal touches—bits of fringe and florals, cozy throws and pillows, and wallpaper galore.

When it came time to make a menu for the tavern, Tim's culinary concept was a perfect match for Eliza's design ethos: "Timeless, never trendy, simple but rustic," he says. "The goal was not to modernize, nor was it to go fully traditional." Just like Eliza and Tim themselves, their decor and dishes would fit together flawlessly, her velvet and marble complemented by his Cornish game hen and fried fingerling potatoes.

It took two long years to complete, and, somehow, they even managed to make the process romantic. "So many nights, it was just Tim and me here, a mattress on the floor, a bottle of wine uncorked," Eliza says. "In a lot of ways, it was my favorite time here." They are still smitten—with each other, and now too, with their sweet little Lost Fox Inn. Every day may not be a honeymoon, but it's close, for the couple as well as their guests, who can feel the love for themselves in every cozy, fringed, and floral nook. "We poured our heart and soul into every little thing here," Eliza says. "And when people come and appreciate it and feel at home in it, it's like we're sharing that love with them too."

Above: Eliza and Tim discovered the portrait of the lady in red at a favorite antique shop. "She perfectly represents the design style we were creating for the inn, from her relaxed pose to the gorgeous colors and patterns in the textiles," Eliza says.

Opposite: Forging a sense of history in the main entry was achieved through texture and pattern: a velvet love seat topped with suzani textile pillows, Roman clay walls with classic sconces, and clay brick tilework.

THE POETRY OF SPACES
GROUPIES
LINDA McCARTNEY

LOST FOX

Opposite: In the tavern's powder room are House of Hackney wallpaper and a custom sink basin inked by Eliza in permanent marker.

Above: In the main inn's guest rooms, carpet was replaced with wide-plank wood floors. All the rugs are vintage Turkish sourced from Etsy and local antique shops.

Clockwise from top left: No detail left behind: Lost Fox Inn matchbooks and hydrangeas from the inn's gardens; at the refreshment station, dusty pink cabinets with brass hardware and a matching farmhouse sink that will patina over time; a handsome fox cap on the stairs' newel post.

Clockwise from top left:
The tavern was constructed in 1745 and relocated to this site in 1926; the tavern's potato gnocchi, made with mushrooms, local tomatoes, and corn from a nearby farm in Litchfield; the inn's fox theme plays out in details like the taxidermied red fox behind the front desk.

Above: The moody woodland surrounding the inn was part of the inspiration for the name: "We imagined a little fox rambling through the woods, looking for his way home," Eliza says.

Opposite: Eliza and Tim repaired the eighteenth-century schoolhouse's original beadboard panels and added classic shutters and a lantern pendant. The tub is from Vintage Tub & Bath.

It's a

Beautiful Life

THE GEORGE

Montclair, New Jersey

They say when one door closes, another opens. Rarely, however, do the two events happen in the same day. But in 2016, just as beauty mogul Bobbi Brown was closing the door on a twenty-two-year career at Estée Lauder, her husband, Steven Plofker, invited her to step through her next one. It led to an inn.

To hear Bobbi tell it, that day went something like this: "I called Steven from my office and told him I was leaving Bobbi Brown Cosmetics, and he immediately came out to meet me in the city," she recalls. "He told me he had bought a building and said, 'Why don't we turn it into a hotel?'" Never mind that the couple had never dreamed of, or even talked about, becoming hoteliers. "It was the first time I heard words like that come out of his mouth," Bobbi says. "I looked at him and said, 'Let's do it.'"

Steven, a prominent entrepreneur and real estate developer who owns and has renovated numerous buildings in the couple's hometown of Montclair, New Jersey, had long been circling the stately estate on tree-lined North Mountain Avenue. Constructed in 1902 as a private residence, the Georgian-style structure had been granted landmark status in 2008. Among the commuter town's impressive homes, nearly all of them perched on hilltop lawns trimmed with blossoming hydrangea, it was a neighborhood icon. The house had been operating as The Georgian Inn since the 1970s, and for years, Steven had courted its owner, who remained noncommittal—until one fateful day. "He had entertained a few other offers that had fallen through, and he called me and asked if my offer

Bobbi Brown & Steven Plofker

was still on the table," Steven recalls. "I said, 'I'll buy it tomorrow.'" The timing could only be kismet. Bobbi still had a few years left on a noncompete agreement with her former employer that prohibited her from starting any beauty brands. Why not run out the clock with a new creative endeavor? So what if the couple didn't know the first thing about making a hotel? They had built Bobbi Brown Cosmetics together on gut instinct, banking on natural makeup at a time when red lipstick was all the rage, and there was no denying that they'd been outrageously successful. They'd do it again.

And so it was in this familiar can-do spirit that the couple embarked on their first hotel: as outsiders, keen to stay on the outside and do everything differently—their way—combining Steven's real estate and renovation acumen with Bobbi's artistic savvy. Things started off on the right note: the bones were good, and many historic details—the grand double-staircase, the dentil moldings, the exquisite stained-glass window panels—were remarkably preserved. Sure, the wallpaper was peeling, the carpet threadbare, but all of that was cosmetic. When Steven brought Bobbi to see the inn for the first time, however, she didn't quite share the same vision. "It was pretty rough," she says. "But I have enough understanding and faith that when Steven says something can be done, it can be done."

Steven and Bobbi played to their strengths, with Steven spearheading the construction and Bobbi dreaming up the decor. He focused on the big picture. She targeted the fine details. And every decision was made together. While Bobbi was picking out fabric and paint swatches, Steven was moving mountains—or, at least, buildings: months into the renovation, he orchestrated the relocation of the inn's Queen Anne-style carriage house, moving the 640,000-pound structure from the back of the inn to a street-front lot roughly fifty feet away. Local media turned out for the monumental feat, which Steven casually says, "wasn't that hard. It's not as difficult as it sounds." (Bobbi remains impressed. "That is *so* Steven," she says.)

Structural hurdles cleared, the couple set to work renovating the interiors. Wall upon wall of Sheetrock and plaster was removed, revealing handsome brick. Fireplaces were added in half a dozen rooms. The grand staircase's handcrafted scrollwork and balusters were restored. All the while, Steven and Bobbi collected furniture from antique shops, favorite designers, and even their own homes. The couple amassed so much, they filled an entire warehouse, "and we had no idea where any of it was going," Bobbi says.

When it came time to number the guest rooms, Steven addressed a hotel gripe from the couple's years of traveling. "I am so tired of hotels that have numbered rooms—first floor, second room. Ok, you're room 102," he says. "Enough already!" The couple had already decided to rename the inn The George—cuter and punchier than The Georgian Inn, they thought—so why not give all the rooms their own special moniker too? They started at the beginning of the alphabet: Alex, Bob, Cody, David. In each room, they lined the walls with portraits and iconic photographs of famous people who share that name. In Olivia, Olivia Newton-John takes pride of place above the bed; there's also Liv Tyler, John Oliver, and, cleverly, Laurence Olivier. Three rooms were named for the couple's sons: Dylan, Duke, and Cody. (There is no Bobbi, but there is a Steve—not a Steven.)

For the finishing touches, Bobbi and Steven again turned to their own travels for guidance. In the library, a candy closet was installed, borrowed from a candy room the couple encountered at a resort in the Bahamas. An honor bar was created,

PEACE
AND
HARMONY
DRAWBERTSON

Page 28: The library displays Bobbi and Steven's eclectic style with thrifted lamps, leather chandeliers, and cozy oversized armchairs.

Previous: Bobbi and Steven modernized the reception space with a Timothy Oulton table lamp and a graffiti-style painting of George Washington by Jay Jamil.

Above: Bobbi and Steven with their dog Pippa in the hotel's entry, which is lined with original mosaic tile.

inspired by some of their favorite boutique hotels in Europe. Other in-room amenities were borne of Bobbi's personal favorites in her everyday life: Smeg mini-fridges, Dyson hairdryers, and Nespresso coffeemakers, "because I hate having to get dressed for a good cup of coffee," Bobbi says.

Two years of renovations later, The George opened its doors. And there, behind every new door, in every corner, Bobbi and Steven's touch is felt. Their colors—red, navy, white, and black—inspired largely by the Union Jack and Bobbi's love of the UK, cascade from room to room, playing out in the tartan headboards, throws and accent pillows, and the library's glass cabinets, now filled with personal effects like favorite fragrances, autographed memorabilia, and souvenirs from trips to London.

The closer you look, the more you catch on to the couple's personality—and their sense of humor: the portrait of George Costanza from *Seinfeld* photographed in a compromising burlesque pose, boxers and ankle socks only, leaning against the mantel of the library's fireplace; the dictionary and thesaurus Bobbi gifted Steven for their first wedding anniversary; the painted portraits of dogs in the hallway, part of the couple's personal collection. (So rapacious is Steven and Bobbi's love for their pets, they've created an entire program of amenities for The George's four-legged guests.)

You get the sense that this is their world, and you're just lucky enough to make yourself at home in it for a time, eating all their candy, drinking their wine (none of which they will charge you for, by the way—"It creates a much more homey, collegial atmosphere that way," Steven says), and putting your feet up on their leather sofa, just like Bobbi does.

As it turns out, The George was a great way to ride out Bobbi's noncompete. In 2020, on the very day that contract expired, she launched clean makeup brand Jones Road. But that doesn't mean the couple has closed the door on its inn-keeping chapter. You'll still find them regularly walking the hotel, moving furniture, debating the placement of this lamp or that chair, adding another bit or bauble from a recent London trip. At breakfast, which takes place in the dining room (aka Alex—lined with portraits of Trebek, Ocasio-Cortez, and, of course, The Great), you might bump into Bobbi, who often stops by after her morning walk with the couple's dog, Pippa. Of course, she can't help but chat up the guests. "I like to strike up a conversation, find out where they come from, hear their stories," she says.

And many guests do come with stories. Susan Sarandon, Diane Keaton, Bridget Moynahan, Florence Pugh, Zac Efron, and other Hollywood stars have stayed at the hotel while filming movies nearby. When Steven Spielberg directed *West Side Story* in neighboring Paterson in 2019, he stayed in Cody for the duration of that shoot, regularly taking his dinner in the library and making good use of the blackout curtains after long nights on set.

Even as Bobbi and Steven move into new projects—a Williams Sonoma collaboration, a memoir, and Jones Road brick-and-mortar shops among them—The George will never be fully done for the couple. "We could never stop because we both care so much about every little thing," Bobbi says. "It's never going to be 100 percent finished," Steven agrees. Good thing, Bobbi says. "I don't ever want it to be finished."

ED, FRANK, & HARRY
GUEST ROOMS
FRANCA
WILLIAM WEGMAN
TOP DOGS
GUCCI

37

Previous: The inn's grand double staircase and stained-glass windows were in remarkable condition.

Opposite: The library's original wood paneling was painted a moody slate gray. Red and blue case goods on the mantel are from The George X Williams Sonoma Home collection.

Above: Bobbi and Steven pay homage to many Georges at the inn, from Washington to Clinton in the lobby, to *Seinfeld*'s Costanza in the library.

Clockwise from above: Built in 1902 for a prominent local family, the Georgian-style estate is a Montclair landmark; the ornate details of the staircase required only a fresh coat of paint; Bobbi and Steven's love for pups extends to their collection of dog portraiture—and the inn's pet-friendly policy. "We have dog beds, bandannas, water bowls, snacks—we even have dog walkers available," Bobbi says.

Clockwise from top left:
The vintage trunk bearing a crown insignia was an obvious fit for the Harry room, which also includes a royal plaid headboard and portraits of Prince Harry; a gift shop selling hotel swag is tucked behind another George Washington portrait; the inn's generous breakfast spreads are a source of great pride. "We use as many local suppliers as we can," Steven says. "You can usually find one of us there for breakfast," Bobbi adds.

The Once and

Future Kingdom

GLENMERE MANSION

Chester, New York

The approach to Glenmere Mansion is, in a word, dramatic. Just beyond the quiet country road, past the wrought-iron gates, an expansive lawn unfurls like a royal green carpet. And way up in the distance, glimpsed through sun-dappled leaves dancing on the branches of giant maple trees? A century-old estate, pretty in pink with turquoise shutters. At first, it's on your right, then as you circle up the drive, it's on your left, growing ever grander with each passing second. You could come here a thousand times and the magic of it would never diminish. The word seems to swirl around in the air like fairy dust: *Glenmere* . . .

Drama was built into Glenmere Mansion's very bones, infused by its first owner, Robert Wilson Goelet. The name Goelet may not ring quite as familiar as, say, Vanderbilt or Rockefeller, but during the nineteenth and early twentieth centuries, it carried just as much weight. Descended from the French Huguenots, the Goelets became American aristocracy when they arrived in New York City in the seventeenth century, then capitalist royalty when they established the Chemical Bank in 1824. Third-generation Goelet, Robert Wilson, a banker and real estate developer, built Glenmere Mansion in 1911 as the kind of Xanadu that wealthy families of the day considered part and parcel to their very existence, and it had all the trappings of old-money grandiosity: vaulted ceilings and arched walkways in heaving stone, proper English gardens with burbling fountains and exquisite wrought-iron details, and, of course, that breathtaking, braggadocious, utterly dramatic approach.

Alan Stenberg & Daniel DeSimone

By the time Daniel DeSimone happened upon it in 2006, Glenmere Mansion was nearing its centennial—and though still grand, it was exceedingly rough around the edges. But Dan, recently retired from his orthopedic surgery practice, saw through rose-colored glasses the glimmers of his next big project. He immediately called his real estate agent—and his husband, Alan Stenberg.

"Dan said, 'I found this great villa!'" Alan recalls. "And I thought, 'Oh boy, he's lost it.' It took him two months to get me there because I just didn't believe it: an Italian villa in Chester?" Alan hardly made it up the estate's winding drive before his mind had changed. Even with the English topiaries all but dried up and dead, the Renaissance Revival statues crumbling and covered in dirt, it was evident there was serious pedigree here. The architecture was the work of Carrère and Hastings, the New York society firm behind the Frick Residence and the New York Public Library—and the mansion still carried many an echo of those famed projects: the grand staircase, the beautiful tilework, the extravagant moldings (some severely water damaged but impressive nonetheless). The gardens, though overgrown and in need of revival, were the design of Beatrix Farrand, landscape architect of the Peggy Rockefeller Rose Garden at the New York Botanical Gardens. And discovered glued to the walls of the inner courtyard: not one but two giant, original paintings by American Impressionist J. Alden Twachtman.

There was no denying this was a diamond in the rough. But there was just one problem, Alan recalls. "It was way too big for us!" Dan was way ahead of him, suggesting not a home for two, but an inn for many. "He said, 'I'll cook, you can manage the front of house and change the beds.'" Alan agreed to everything—except changing the beds.

Within months, the couple had closed on their ninety-five acres of heaven and were on the hunt for an interior designer. Alan had plenty of contacts from his days running a fashion PR firm, and for this, he started at the top, calling in heavy hitter Scott Snyder. "We thought there was no way we could afford him," Alan says, recalling the dreary winter day when he and Dan arranged to meet the designer at the mansion—and Snyder arrived in a white stretch limousine. "But he instantly connected with the project," Alan says. This room would be dark and sexy; that one, bright and vibrant. "He got it. He was in all the way."

Renovations took nothing short of a village. The crew of more than 120 worked six days a week—sometimes seven—with Dan and Alan at their side. On any given day, you could find a team of octogenarian restorers teetering on ladders, carefully repairing the water-damaged moldings; Pennsylvania Dutch woodworkers stripping and staining every original door and panel; artisans painting elaborate *verre églomisé* for the dining room and carefully extracting those Twachtman murals; and three teams of craftsmen installing miles of marble in the twenty new bathrooms. "We needed so much marble, it ended up making more sense to acquire a small interest in an Italian quarry than to buy it outright," Alan says.

All the while, Dan and Alan scoured auction catalogs and antique shops, a pastime they already coveted as longtime collectors of china, art, books, and furniture. Now they trained their talents on unearthing exceptional finds in the spirit of Glenmere, acquiring paintings and photographs of the Goelet clan—black-and-white portraits of Mary Goelet, the Duchess of Roxburghe; a reproduction of John Singer Sargent's oil painting of baby Beatrice Goelet—along with modern works from the private

Page 42: The mansion's grand entrance features a dramatic stone entry, original iron sconces, and, flanking the door, a pair of dog statues.

Previous: A painting depicting a Venice ball was one of two large works by J. Alden Twachtman found glued to the walls of the mansion's cortile.

Above: The private courtyard is filled with manicured topiaries, Renaissance-style statues, and cherub fountains.

collection of friends (and silent investors) Alison and Peter Klein, and more contemporary furnishings. The idea, says Alan, was not a single design ethos but an accumulative aesthetic, "Like a family estate that has been built on over the generations."

When it came time to paint the exterior of the mansion, Dan and Alan felt an initial sense of obligation to adhere strictly to Glenmere's original color scheme of pink walls with green shutters. But once complete, the shade applied to the walls appeared more "ointment pink," in Dan's words, than rosy Mediterranean. A timely—and costly—salt-wash treatment was applied to create a patina more appropriately provincial. Green shutters, meanwhile, didn't feel right—"Too heavy, not cheerful enough," Alan says. Decision-fatigued after what had become three grueling years of intense renovations, the couple shelved the dilemma for another day, instead packing their bags for a much-needed vacation to Italy.

Like all good epiphanies, the solution to their shutter quandary hit them suddenly and out of the literal blue: As they arrived at their hotel, Rome's lavish Hotel de Russie, who but a *very* famous Hollywood couple exited the front doors . . . just as Alan was admiring the hotel's Mediterranean-blue shutters. "It's a sign!" he exclaimed to Dan. (And perhaps it really *was* a sign: years later, the very same Hollywood couple inquired about a free stay at Glenmere Mansion. "We politely declined," Alan says with a smile.)

Shutters sorted, back from holiday, the couple's work was done. Glenmere Mansion was reborn. Now they had an inn to run.

In the early days, they were lucky if they had three weekend bookings during the high season. Word spread slowly at first, then rapidly, almost overnight. "A magazine ran an article about us and suddenly we had five hundred calls in one weekend," Alan recalls. "I was still writing the reservations down on a piece of paper and handing them to my assistant. We were completely overwhelmed, in a good way."

Fifteen years later, Glenmere Mansion isn't just a well-oiled machine; it is in its next heyday. The gardens have grown tall and thick, the lawns are lush. A spa, pool, tennis courts, and wedding venue have been added, along with more land to total two hundred acres. Dan planted a rose garden and went to bee school—"A crowning achievement that even beats medical school," Alan laughs. A chicken coop and vegetable garden were installed and today supply fresh eggs and produce for the inn's copious breakfast spreads.

In the end, Alan did change a few beds, though there's a housekeeping team for that now. And while Dan cooked at first, a full-time chef has been hired to oversee multicourse dinners that draw gourmands from throughout the Northeast. These days, the couple tend to think of themselves as stewards of the next generation of Glenmere royalty, extending a warm welcome to guests who eat, drink, sleep, and play like modern-day Goelets. "There is a romantic side to all of this that just takes over your senses—and your life," Alan says thoughtfully, perching on the marble steps of the mansion's entrance, flanked by a pair of dutiful dog statues. "If we had thought about all that it would take, if we had really spent enough time thinking about what we were getting ourselves into, we probably never would have done it." Then, looking around the kingdom he's built, he adds, "Thank god we kept our rose-colored glasses on."

Opposite: The design concept for the Frog's End Tavern was loosely inspired by one of Alan and Dan's favorite bars, the Hotel Belles Rives' Piano Bar Fitzgerald, in the Cote d'Azur.

Above: The first attempt to recreate the mansion's original pink walls was less than successful. A salt wash treatment was applied to achieve the right shade and patina.

Top left and right: Alan and Dan opted for "Mediterranean-blue" shutters—a departure from the mansion's original color scheme that was inspired by a visit to the Hotel de Russie in Rome; Alan looking dapper in front of Glenmere Mansion's grand entrance.

This page and opposite bottom: Re-creations of Beatrix Farrand's gardens were possible after Alan acquired copies of the landscape architect's original plans for Glenmere Mansion from a university in California. "We made a nice donation for those plans," Alan laughs.

Above: Modern works from Alison and Peter Klein's private art museum outside of Stuttgart, Germany, hang in the guest rooms. The couple are family friends and investors in the inn.

Opposite: In the grand living room, Murano glass chandeliers were designed by Alberto Donghia. The original dentil moldings, decorative door casings, and fireplace were painstakingly restored.

Opposite: Decorative artist and restorer Staszek Kotowski created gilded *verre églomisé* screens for the dining room.

Above: Antique Rosenthal fish-patterned plates from Alan and Dan's extensive china collection are arranged on the wall of the private dining room.

Above and opposite: Velvet sofas and silk drapes set the tone in the mansion's library, which interior designer Scott Snyder "wanted dark and sexy," Alan says. The subject of the regal portrait above the sofa is unknown.

The Garden Book

Long Island

The Currency

# of Kindness

THE ROUNDTREE, AMAGANSETT

The Hamptons, New York

Sylvia Wong knows how to solve problems. Real problems. *Big* problems. As general counsel for a global tech giant, she traveled the world with a security detail, leading emerging markets in more than a hundred countries. As a mergers-and-acquisitions attorney for a top-five law firm, she managed cutthroat billion-dollar negotiations on a regular basis. She's an expert litigator. She can hold her own in a room full of screaming, angry men. By all accounts, she is a total badass. "It was a very macho environment," Sylvia says of her career. "I was always one of the only women in a room full of men with strong personalities, but I realized you don't have to be loud to be heard."

Her quiet confidence took her far—all the way to Asia, along with her husband and son, to oversee her company's global expansion. She lived in Singapore, then Shanghai. When she wasn't crisscrossing the globe for work, she was doing it for fun: Easter Island, Venice, the Galápagos Islands, the Atacama Desert. Sometimes it was ultraluxurious; other times, not so much. "In some of the emergent markets where we did business, the hotels were so gritty, I'd use my jacket to open the door." But no matter. Every experience was a new perspective to be appreciated. "The top five memories in my life—all of them are related to travel."

In 2012, Sylvia returned to New York City, and a few years later, traded in for a somewhat less demanding role as a partner in a private investment firm. Suddenly, there was time to think. And what kept coming back to her was the joy of travel, her love of hotels, and all the small things that fed her soul when she experienced a new

Sylvia Wong

place. She had always adored little inns and hideaways. Who better than Sylvia to become the ultimate innkeeper?

She began to search—but for what exactly? A property in Palm Springs? A little place in Sicily? No, it would have to be somewhere closer to home. Perhaps she'd convert a row of townhouses in the city. Then, one winter day, she stumbled upon the Gansett Green Manor. Sylvia had spent many summers in the Hamptons, but this fourteen-room inn on Amagansett's picturesque Main Street was entirely new to her.

Within a week she had hopped the jitney from Manhattan and found herself dropped directly across the street from the Gansett Green's century-old barn. The owners, a lovely couple ready to retire, showed her around. Inside, the condition left something to be desired, with motel-style kitchenettes in each room—but as the owners led her deeper into the property, Sylvia realized this was no mere inn; this was an estate. Half a dozen cedar-shingled cottages dotted the two-acre grounds, and at the center, a sprawling lawn that felt to Sylvia like a secret oasis. It was the Green Gansett's green haven that ultimately sold her on it. The papers were signed, and by the summer, Sylvia was a bona fide innkeeper.

When the first nips of autumnal chill rolled in, Sylvia shuttered the Gansett Green for renovations. By now, her vision was clear: "The idea was to treat it as I would treat my house and create the entire experience to make our guests feel as if this is our home, as well as their home." There would be no dressing up, no clichéd Hamptons pretensions to speak of, but there would be beautiful things, luxurious things—"The kinds of things expected by high achievers, very demanding, type A people—which is me!" Working with an architect, she bid the project out to more than half a dozen contractors. All of them returned with estimates that were three to four times her budget. This was a problem—but Sylvia had certainly seen bigger problems in her day. She'd find someone else.

Enter Carlos. A young contractor still establishing his business, he came highly recommended by an acquaintance who had used him for a home renovation. His estimate was right on the money—but he admitted he had never taken on a project of this scale before. Well, neither had Sylvia. With her architect, they went page by page through the project, and by the time they reached the end, she was certain he could handle the job. "And I'll tell you what," she says. "Our first major task was to finish the demo. We budgeted three weeks to get it done, and Carlos finished in less than a week." He clearly understood the assignment.

Alas, more setbacks lay just up the road. By the third week, the team discovered the cottages had no foundation. It was an impressive problem considering the structures had managed to stay firmly standing for nearly a century—and it necessitated an equally impressive solution. Sylvia had two options: either lift the houses by crane and build a foundation beneath them, or go the old-fashioned route, by hand, and dig the foundations section by section. She didn't have the budget for the former, but with Carlos's team, she had the manpower for the latter. "So, we did it the primitive way," she says—and all the time they'd saved in demo was instantly gobbled up.

Then another, even bigger hurdle came along: COVID. Work came to a screeching halt. This roadblock looked like a dead end. But Sylvia, ever the power litigator, had an epiphany: If hotels were considered essential businesses, shouldn't the construction of a hotel be as well? With the local

66

Page 62: The century-old barn—now a spacious guest house—presides over Amagansett's Main Street, at the entrance to the inn.

Previous: A casual ease is ever-present at The Roundtree. "I want guests to feel like they are staying with family or friends, and always well taken care of," Sylvia says.

Above: Sylvia was drawn to the estate's expansive lawns dotted with historic cedar-shingled cottages, all hidden away behind Main Street.

government in disarray, Sylvia had no recourse but to send what felt like a message in a bottle. "I just emailed the address on the New York State website," she says. Within a few weeks, she had convinced the state to grant her permission to restart construction. She emailed the documentation to her lawyer, furnished a copy to the town officials and police chief, and posted her exemption on the inn's front door. "With a bit of stubbornness and optimism, as well as my lawyering skills, miracles can happen," she says. At last, they were on a roll. And though problems still arose—materials were in short supply, social distancing slowed progress—Sylvia batted them away with her dogged tenacity and keen powers of persuasion.

When it came time to decorate the inn, Sylvia turned to the makers and artists she had long surrounded herself with at home: Denmark's Vipp for midcentury chairs and modular sofas, Italy's Salvatori and Desalto for more furnishings, and favorite artists such as Italian Franco Passalacqua and Australian Janine Mackintosh for original works to hang on the walls. She even added her own immaculately designed Hamptons beach house to the inn's pool of rooms.

On June 1, 2020, Sylvia opened her inn, right on schedule. In front of the old, shingled barn—now freshly painted and decorated—she placed a crisp white square reading *The Roundtree, Amagansett*. The new name could have easily referenced the topiary-style trees at the edge of the inn's great lawn, but in fact, it was an homage to Dovey Johnson Roundtree, the civil rights activist and attorney who won the first bus desegregation case against the Interstate Commerce Commission in 1955. "I admire her courage and grit," Sylvia says.

In the spirit of her "home away from home" concept, Sylvia insisted that nearly everything would be on the house: the minibars and the daily breakfast, afternoon tea and late-night snacks, even laundry service. "If you're my guest, I really want to take care of you," she says. "I want to spoil you." Even with that nurturing nature, Sylvia still saw her role as a transactional one. Only after The Roundtree welcomed its first visitors did she begin to see it as something else . . . something emotional. It started with an early guest—a prominent local doctor—who was so impressed with his experience that he immediately sent his well-heeled friends for stays of their own. Over the years, others—leaders of *Fortune* 500 companies, even a board member of her former employer—were similarly taken with Sylvia's creation, sending her thank-you letters and gifts, and returning again and again, always with the warm familiarity of an old friend. Certainly, she had expected her Hamptons clientele to enjoy her inn, but never had she imagined they'd return her hospitality with kindnesses of their own. "That still surprises me to this day," she says. "I didn't expect the warmth to come back to me."

What endears these discerning guests to The Roundtree is hard to put into words. The lawyer in Sylvia is likely to point out the excellent amenities, the luxurious appointments, the perfectly manicured gardens and lawn (and she'd be accurate in doing so). But the innkeeper in Sylvia has another theory. "It's the generosity of spirit, the human connection," she says. "That's not something you write into a business plan, but it's why I feel so fortunate to have this place."

JERUSALEM
LongHouse

Opposite: Sylvia added her own vacation home—built in the 1960s by pioneering Hamptons architect Alfred Scheffer for the playwright Neil Simon—to the inn's inventory of accommodations. The double-sided brick fireplace is original.

Above: In the main house, a painting by one of Sylvia's favorite artists, Italian Franco Passalacqua, hangs above fireplace.

Clockwise from above: Though there was plenty of room on the grand lawn, Sylvia opted not to install a pool at the inn. "Hamptons people go to the beach. I'm there every morning. That's what I want for my guests too," she says; breakfast is a feast for the eyes as well as the stomach; beach cruisers are another amenity encouraging guests to experience the Hamptons like locals.

Clockwise from top left:
The vases in the guest rooms were custom made for The Roundtree by Balinese ceramicist Kevala; Sylvia's own tea set, a collection of handmade pieces from Japan and the Hamptons; a wall of buoys on one of the Beach House's terraces.

Opposite: Sylvia keeps The Roundtree's lush gardens meticulously landscaped, and regularly arrives with fresh flowers from Amber Waves Farm, just down the street.

Above: The house car—a baby-blue Moke—is perfect for beach days and jaunts around the Hamptons.

Serendipity and

Sprezzatura

SILVER SANDS MOTEL & BEACH BUNGALOWS

Greenport, New York

The first time Alexander Perros turned down Silvermere Road, he was motivated by nothing more than curiosity. The street was marked by a sign that piqued his interest: "Silver Sands Motel," it read, its capital S's formed from the curving outline of a big blue seahorse. Down the long wooded lane, he passed a bog full of croaking toads, crossed over train tracks, and skirted a saltwater marsh where cranes and egrets perched gracefully. And then, crowned by blue-and-red neon at the end of the road, was Silver Sands.

Alex and his wife, Anna, had recently purchased a weekend home nearby, and this discovery felt like kismet. He was instantly captivated by the frozen-in-time motel, which he learned dated back to the 1950s. "It was completely serendipitous, but when I saw it, there was just something about it," he says. He wasn't the only one who thought so: despite being run down, the place was nearly full. Sure, most guests brought their own sheets—even their own cleaning supplies—but they were as loyal as could be, most of them regulars for decades. "It had so much presence, so much charm, so much history. There was this unexplainable attraction." Alex asked a local friend, a broker, if the owner might consider an offer. Not a chance, came the unequivocal answer. It was still owned by the family that had opened it, and they'd never sell. Alex told her to give him a call if that ever changed.

In January 2020, the call came: the motel's second-generation proprietor had passed away, and his sister, then in her seventies, was running the place on a shoestring budget. The family might be inclined to sell after all.

Alexander Perros

The timing was perfect. Alex had recently left his role as president at Lindsey Adelman Studio, and having found some success in real estate development, was looking for a new project that would satisfy both sides of his brain—a business endeavor that would allow him to flex his creative muscles. He put in an offer.

But what came next was anything but easy. "I walked into an unbelievable family feud," Alex says. It would become a saga worthy of a novel, a subject of endless speculation around town. Two years would pass before tenacity and patience finally won out: in April 2022, Silver Sands was his.

The very next day, Alex arrived to assess his new motel. The last guests had just made their departure. Rooms were left in disarray; the coffee in the kitchenettes had barely gone cold. In the following days and weeks, he opened every door, looking under every floorboard and behind every wall, collecting furniture for recycling and tossing abandoned bric-a-brac (a machete was among the more unusual leftovers). As he chipped away at the clutter, slowly revealing the bones of the motel, he came to realize this would not be a quick scrape-and-paint job. The plumbing was leaky. The interior walls of the motel were rotted. Downed power lines were strewn about the overgrown lawns. In some of the foundations, he discovered water—never a good thing, but especially bad when there's enough for fish to swim in it. "Smart money would have said tear the whole thing down," Alex says. "But I felt protective."

Often, as Alex wandered the grounds, people would turn up—former guests, curious to know for themselves what would become of their favorite haunt. One day, a woman showed up looking distressed. "She held her hands over her chest, and I could just tell she was upset," he says. She recounted that she had vacationed in one of the cottages for years with her family. On one visit, she recalled to him, her mother made a painting of a vase her father had decorated with seashells plucked from the Silver Sands beach. After that, the family brought the painting with them on every summer vacation.

Alex walked with the woman to the cottage, which by then had been thoroughly stripped, and there, miraculously, hanging on the shiplap paneling above the fireplace, was the painting. Affixed to the back was a photo of the woman's mother, sitting on the beach, a copy of *The New York Post* spread across her lap, a floppy fuchsia hat shading her face. "So, she starts crying, and that makes me start crying," Alex recalls. He gave her the painting; she gave him the photo of her mother. And before the woman left, he told her he would honor her mother's memory. "I just kept thinking this woman in the photograph *is* Silver Sands."

Alex took the encounter as a sign—*the sign* that would ultimately mold the motel's future. He would not re-create Silver Sands so much as escort it into its next chapter. It would be reborn, a palimpsest of everything it had been before, with dashes of the new and modern—yet still germane—sprinkled throughout. But first, the canvas needed to be cleared.

Tackling the U-shaped motel structure was another moment of serendipity. As contrators studied the building, they realized it was composed of an inner and outer shell. None of the interior walls were load bearing, and dropped ceilings inexplicably obscured the outer shell's beautiful vaulting. Unusual as it all was, it was a godsend, allowing Alex to remove every interior wall and ceiling at once without compromising the structural integrity.

Landscaping, meanwhile, became a pivotal point in the property's evolution. The beach, unmaintained, had over the previous winter become a mud pit "so deep it would suck your

Page 74: The lobby was transformed from a cramped wood-paneled reception desk to a light-filled space where guests gather from sunrise to late night.

Previous: Rather than create a new aesthetic, Alex remained faithful to the motel's 1950s vibe—including its salmon-pink and sea-blue facades.

Above: Silver Sands's private beach was expanded, and the scalloped orange umbrellas were brought over from Italy.

shoe right off," Alex recalls. The oaks and London planes throughout were overgrown and in the courtyard of the motel, giant juniper trees had grown so unruly, they blocked out the views, the beach—even the sunshine. "They were like something out of Dr. Seuss." He hired landscape architect Edmund D. Hollander to make sense of it all, and little by little, trees were trimmed and native plants, shrubs, and flowers brought in to fill out the grounds. More sand was added to the existing shoreline, too, enhancing its 1,400 feet of golden beach overlooking Peconic Bay. Things were coming alive, as if the old motel was reanimating before his eyes.

The canvas reinvigorated, it was time to put a fresh spin on what was left. Alex settled on a single word for inspiration: *sprezzatura*. The Italian concept—roughly, the art of effortless grace—was the basis for Silver Sands' entire ethos. "It is casual, not too done," he wrote in a mini manifesto. "It is a feeling of knowing it is chic and cool but without being self-conscious about it." Sprezzatura plays out most evidently on the beach, where the retro sun loungers and scalloped orange umbrellas come from Italy—very 1960s Amalfi Coast. It also sets the tone for the interiors, an updated blend of midcentury modern styles. Outside, red geraniums were planted in window boxes, and 1950s French art deco–style patio chairs were nestled among the pampas grass lining the lawn.

Next came the restaurants. On the edge of the beach, a bar was constructed around one of the property's largest oaks, with old fisherman baskets hanging from the branches and funky teal tile—the motel's original floors—topping the counter. White patio furniture was dropped right into the sand for barefoot alfresco meals of fresh oysters (farmed steps away, right off the Silver Sands beach), ceviche, and other locavore delights. Nookies Diner, meanwhile, took the role of faithfully retro classic counter, short-order menu and all. "It's groovy, it's cool," Alex says. And on one wall, in colorful Warhol-esque screenprints, reading *The New York Post* on the beach, the woman who came to represent the soul of Silver Sands to Alex.

Today, Silver Sands comes together "like jazz," Alex says—effortlessly, naturally, always evolving, and never taking itself too seriously . . . *Sprezzatura*. That casual coolness has inevitably lured a new crowd, but more importantly to Alex, it has drawn the longtime regulars who spent every summer on these shores and are now old enough to bring their own children and grandchildren. "Even though this place has changed, the fact that they came back means everything," he says. "It tells me I got it right. Maybe I changed Silver Sands, but more than anything, Silver Sands completely changed me."

Above left and opposite: The lobby is a cheerful complement to the punchy turquoise and salmon of the motel's exterior. Seashell art is by Lucie de Moyencourt.

Above right: Alex spent an entire summer restoring the original Silver Sands neon sign in the barn behind the motel.

Opposite and above left: Eddie's, an airy, alfresco restaurant and bar on the sand, pairs masterful seafood creations with wood-fired Neapolitan pies.

Above right: A mixed-media print using archival photography of Silver Sands hangs above a daybed in one of the motel rooms.

Above: Alex and his wife, Anna, designed the beach houses with vintage pieces and custom built-ins, like Casa de Buddy's pine bench with its colorful cushions.

Opposite: The Casa de Buddy bungalow is an homage to the '70s, with a rattan elephant side table in the style of Vivai del Sud and a de Sede DS-600 sofa.

Clockwise from above:
Alex replicated the window boxes of red geraniums that were a fixture of the original motel; nostalgic motel-style key chains "have our address printed on the back," Alex says. "Drop a key in any mailbox and it will find its way back to us;" Nookies Diner is a repository for motel memorabilia, including a series of screenprints made by artist Kris VandeWalle from the photo that inspired much of Alex's vision for the inn.

Clockwise from top left: Nookies Diner features an original Silver Sands sign bearing the iconic blue seahorse; the donut of the day and fresh coffee at Nookies; Eddie's ceviche, served in a coconut half on the restaurant's bar, which is topped with repurposed tile from the motel's rooms.

Upstate

Euro

Vision

EASTWIND HOTELS

Lake Placid, New York | Big Indian, New York | Windham, New York

They met the summer of 2010 at a hotel on Shelter Island. The setting couldn't have been more idyllic: sunset beach parties, DJs spinning, an endless supply of oysters and rosé. Except all that was for everyone *but* Julija Stoliarova. "I was managing the hotel restaurant, and it was nonstop," she recalls. "It was breakfast, lunch, and dinner—six in the morning until midnight."

But there was a bright side: Bjorn Boyer. It was Bjorn's fourth summer working at the hotel, albeit in the relatively mellow back-of-house environs of the finance department, and in between Julija's long and hectic hours, somehow the two found time to get to know each other.

She was born and raised in Lithuania and had arrived in the United States as a model after walking the runways of Europe and Japan. He grew up outside of Berlin and played semiprofessional soccer before attending college in Connecticut. They found they had similar sensibilities—both were outdoorsy, ambitious, and industrious—and were naturals in their respective roles at the hotel. Julija had realized her proclivity for hospitality through restaurants after she pivoted from modeling to hostessing soon after landing in New York City. She fit easily into the scene at the city's *it* restaurants, doing face control, rubbing elbows with celebrities, and eventually rising to general manager. Bjorn, meanwhile, climbed the corporate ladder at major hotel brands, running finance and operations.

When that fateful summer ended, Julija and Bjorn moved back to New York City and got an

Bjorn Boyer & Julija Stoliarova

apartment together. And as their careers continued to flourish, they flourished as a couple. After the birth of their second child, Myla, they settled in Montclair, New Jersey, and began to dream of creating something of their own, a project that would blend their hospitality know-how with their appreciation for the great outdoors. The Catskills soon called to them. "There was something familiar about it from both of our backgrounds," Bjorn says. "Beautiful forests, lakes, rivers." Nearly a year of steady searching procured the perfect place: a 1950s motor inn minutes from the chairlifts of Windham Mountain. The condition wasn't great ("Terrible," in fact, says Julija), but the setting was just what the couple was looking for, all rolling hills framed by giant oaks, with acres of raw, untouched nature.

Renovations began in earnest. Bjorn enlisted his mother, an engineer, to help with the architectural drawings, and his father arrived from Germany with a handful of friends to tackle demolition. Dan Cipriani, a fellow hospitality pro and construction guru, joined the couple as a partner. Bjorn, still working his nine-to-five in the city, moonlighted as general contractor, rushing up to Windham every Thursday evening to play weekend warrior, pouring every ounce of energy he could muster into the project before he had to call it quits come Sunday night.

Meanwhile, Julija took the reins on interior design. From the start, her concept was clear—and yet not. "I knew that I wanted it to be warm and inviting. It had to be one-of-a-kind," she says. "My biggest fear was if someone could identify where all the furniture came from. I would die!" She settled on an all-vintage style, with a focus on midcentury Scandinavian design. But where to begin? She started by casting a wide net, attending antique fairs and combing Etsy and Facebook Marketplace. Eventually, she made inroads with dealers and found her knack for curation. "My favorites were the estate sales and church consignment stores," she says. "They always had these unwanted things that I actually really wanted—and they were so excited to sell them to me."

It took nine months to finish the main house, and another two after that to complete the annex. Between the two structures, the couple would operate nineteen rooms, but Bjorn's head for numbers told him it would be more profitable for the business to have at least twenty. Inspiration struck, as it so often does, while scrolling Pinterest: a photo of a Scandinavian A-frame cabin. Bjorn tracked the manufacturer, Lushna, all the way to Slovenia and, in a twist of fate, learned that the company had an American production facility . . . in New York . . . just a few miles from Windham. They commissioned three cabins, and later another seven, which Julija customized to match the vintage feel of the rest of the property. They named the place Eastwind—east of Windham.

With the heavy lifting done, the couple began to home in on the little details. Again and again, they returned to their similar upbringings in Europe. "So much of what we wanted to do was still not very common in America," Julija says. "No televisions in the room, lots of communal spaces, and it was important to us to have a sauna—this is a big part of our culture." Fireplaces and large tables were added indoors and out. Hammocks were hung from the trees. An oversize barrel hot tub and sauna were nestled into a forested nook. It was all designed to encourage people to connect with one another. And they did. Guests—even notoriously insular New Yorkers—immediately took to the social atmosphere. In the winter, they don blanket ponchos and skitter down the hill to the sauna's warm embrace. Year-round, they gather around bonfires to make s'mores. (Alas, Bjorn's attempt to institute *snobrød*, a doughy Danish alternative to the gooey American favorite, didn't catch on.)

Page 96: Cozy cabins with private bonfires are scattered across Eastwind Lake Placid's forested property.

Previous: The Lushna cabins are an upstyled take on Scandinavian camping.

Above: Julija and Bjorn, with Mateo, Myla, and Woods the dog, make s'mores around the bonfire at Eastwind Lake Placid.

By the time they finished Windham, they were ready to do it all over again with a second project. They found it less than thirty miles away in the Catskills' wooded Oliverea Valley. The forty-seven-acre tract in the natural bowl-shaped valley was perfect for another Eastwind retreat.

Julija and Bjorn once again called on Lushna—this time customizing two large structures in addition to A-frame cabins. The first, a double-height slant-roofed building with floor-to-ceiling windows, would operate as a lounge and casual restaurant. The second would house the property's suites. "I loved the fact that Oliverea would be a more modern construction because it was so different than Windham," Bjorn says.

Julija's second great furniture quest commenced immediately. By then, she had a Rolodex of sellers to call on, and she quickly amassed a new collection, this time focused on Danish midcentury—a "more elevated" aesthetic to match the new build's clean lines. "Anything that comes from Denmark has impeccable quality—I don't know how this tiny country does it," she says.

As Eastwind #2 was underway, Eastwind #3 all but fell into the couple's lap. While vacationing in Lake Placid, they fell in love. On a quiet street just outside of town, the couple caught sight of a 1950s motor lodge, fronted by a Victorian building and bordered by a gurgling river. Unfortunately, the property was already under contract—and even more disheartening, the new owner had plans to raze the place. But the following year, the couple returned and discovered that the deal had fallen through. They pounced, and soon found themselves in a very familiar position, preparing to renovate—while continuing to oversee the construction at Oliverea Valley.

The next two years would be a blur, pulling Julija and Bjorn in four opposing directions, between their two Catskills properties, their new Lake Placid acquisition, and their home in Montclair. Crazy as it sounds, there were remarkably few disasters, and though Julija found the newest property to be her greatest design challenge yet—each of its twenty-one rooms across six guesthouses was a unique layout, requiring far more premeditation and planning than before—her 1970s vision for the hotel nonetheless came together.

On August 1, 2022, Eastwind Lake Placid was ready for guests. Eastwind Oliverea Valley opened the following January, right on its heels. It was the end of a marathon of furniture runs and estate sales, backbreaking construction, and never-ending punch lists, hundreds of miles and countless days apart from one another. It was also the beginning of a new family, Lake Placid and Oliverea Valley forming the perfect complements to their first baby in Windham. Like any family, it needs nurturing, and the couple still bounce like a pair of ping-pong balls between their three children (not to mention their real children). But there's a relative calm as the day-to-day now means refining their creations. "We had to figure out a lot of things, no matter if it was financing or design or growth or market segmentation," Bjorn says. "But every hotel, every restaurant, every bar or club we worked in made us who we are, and made Eastwind what it is." Even—or perhaps especially—that fateful summer spot on Shelter Island.

RECEPTION
RESTAURANT & BAR

Previous: At the heart of Eastwind Oliverea Valley's forty-seven acres is a double height slant-roofed main building that houses Dandelion, the couple's farm-to-fork restaurant and bar.

Above: The bar at Dandelion is an airy, plant-filled place for a craft cocktail or local beer.

Opposite: At Oliverea Valley's main lodge, Julija complemented Scandi finds with an antique fireplace and the other half of her Up & Up table. The rounded vintage sofa "was my most prized purchase," she says.

TROUT & SALMON OF THE WORLD
AMERICA THE BEAUTIFUL
THE BEST OF LIFE
Saturday Night Live
anatomy of contemporary furniture
THE WORLD IN 1977
The Associated Press

Left, top and bottom: "We got lucky with the pool at Lake Placid," says Julija. "It just needed to be refinished." The couple added Amalfi-inspired umbrellas and matching pool floats. Above: Julija sits at the bar in Eastwind Lake Placid's reception. The tile is from Portugal.

Clockwise from top left:
The Catskills region's landscape reminded the couple of their upbringings in Germany and Lithuania; breakfast spreads are heavy on fresh local provisions and served in the lounge or hand-delivered to rooms in a picnic basket; Kiva fireplaces, barrel saunas, and bonfires are nestled throughout the grounds of each property.

TO THE CATSKILLS
COMMUNAL DINNERS

Opposite and above: Altogether, Julija purchased three hundred rugs—all vintage and mostly from Turkey. Pendleton was another go-to resource, for patterned quilts, blankets, and ponchos (in lieu of robes).

Opposite and above left: Bjorn and Julija customized cabins and suites with a Slovenia-based fabricator.

Above right: At Eastwind Windham, the couple added a restored Malm fireplace and orange wingback chairs found at an estate sale. The game cube is from Restoration Hardware.

It Takes

a Village

INNS OF AURORA

Aurora, New York

Pleasant Rowland has a habit of going big—huge even. It's almost as if the word *small* is entirely absent from her vocabulary (which is also quite large). Take, for example, American Girl. When she created the doll brand, today the very definition of cultish, she made toy history, elevating the Barbie-and-baby-doll playscape of the 1980s to a new plane of existence—intellectual, diverse, downright addictive. So big was her business by 1998 that she sold it to Mattel for $700 million.

As an art lover, she's perhaps even bigger, known to collect and commission almost obsessively. And as an innkeeper, Pleasant is no different. She couldn't stop at one. No, she quite nearly made a village.

To be fair, Inns of Aurora came to Pleasant—not the other way around. Technically, it all started in 1998, though one could just as easily argue that her innkeeping destiny was written in the stars since her days at Wells College, a private liberal arts school in Aurora, New York. Wells already had a venerable history as one of the first American universities for women, established in 1868 on the shores of picturesque Cayuga Lake. And when Pleasant arrived on its leafy campus as a bright-eyed seventeen-year-old freshman in 1958, she couldn't have been better suited to its dignified reputation. "I was an English major and had very little idea that I would end up in any business," she recalls, "but I was in love with the entire college experience."

Decades and loads of success later, Pleasant was asked to give the keynote at the 1998 graduation ceremony. She happily obliged and, once again

Pleasant Rowland

on campus, discovered that remarkably little had changed since her own school days. "The buildings were in bad shape, the inn where parents stayed was boarded up. I remember the sofa in the lobby of McMillin, the main academic building, had the same orange fabric on it that it did when I was a student," she says with a laugh. "It needed a little bit of sprucing, as they say."

Others might have put it less delicately: The college was in dire straits. And soon, Pleasant realized her invitation to speak had come with an ulterior—if hopeful—motive. "They asked for a donation," she says, "so I wrote them a check." (In saying this, Pleasant exercises exceptional modesty, for this was not a small check. In fact, it was the kind of check that is typically printed across a piece of three-foot-wide cardboard—for $40 million.) But with that check came a condition: creative control. Pleasant would oversee every penny spent through a newly created nonprofit, the Aurora Foundation.

And so, Pleasant did what Pleasant knows best: "I rolled up my sleeves and got to work." Structures were repaired, classrooms remodeled, dorms renovated—and even hung with artwork from her personal collection. The old orange sofa saw its fateful last day in McMillin, and in 2003, the newly renovated Aurora Inn once again welcomed guests.

But that was only the beginning.

Just down the road, Pleasant turned another historic building, a well-preserved circa-1858 stone mansion built by Colonel Edwin Barber Morgan, into another inn. Here, she found a trove of treasures to work with: the original owner's bureau and grand piano; rooms full of antiques, which were repaired and reupholstered; and striking details that would be nearly impossible to re-create today, like the hand-etched skylights and a carved pink marble fireplace. Art was the final coup de grâce: vibrant still-lifes, striking abstracts, exquisite objets sourced from Pleasant's travels around the globe.

By then, nearly a decade had passed since Pleasant's fateful return to Aurora, and though she had leapt headfirst into every detail of E.B. Morgan House and Aurora Inn, she was still not yet a full-fledged innkeeper, as the college continued to own and operate both properties (with generous funding from its fairy godmother, of course). But that would change when, a few years later, Wells returned to, well, the well.

In 2014, the school offered Pleasant a more permanent stake in Aurora—a handful of landmarked buildings dotting the town's elm-lined Main Street. Among them were Zabriskie House, constructed in 1904 for Morgan's grandson, Robert Morgan Zabriskie; the ionic-columned Taylor House, built in 1838 as a prep school; and the stately redbrick Wallcourt Hall, a former student dormitory. Ever the big thinker, Pleasant bought the whole lot, plus the Aurora Inn and E.B. Morgan House.

Like their neighbors, the new acquisitions were in desperate need of some good old-fashioned Pleasant Rowland "sprucing." Working independently this time, she entered the next chapter of her Aurora story with a clear vision: a series of inns, each faithfully restored and augmented by her own beloved possessions. Though she had no formal training as an interior designer, she was decisive and discerning in her taste—"I love color, I love contemporary"—and she was convinced it would balance out the historic homes in just the right way.

At each house, that vision came to fruition in a different style. Her concept for Wallcourt Hall was influenced by a swatch of burnt orange, white, and black fabric, pulled from her extensive textile archive. In the inn's living room, sofas and chairs were upholstered in the fabric, and walls were painted the same nearly red hue to match.

Above: In the grand entry of E.B. Morgan House: The mirror is an antique. The two tole jardinieres that flank it are from Niermann Weeks. The ceiling moldings and Gothic-style pendant light are original.

Opposite: The antique grand piano at E.B. Morgan House is Pleasant's own, made by Adam Schaaf in Chicago.

Opposite and above left: In the main parlor at E.B. Morgan House, a cabinet is filled with Pleasant's yellow Wedgwood china.

Above right: The pink marble fireplace is the centerpiece of the front parlor, formerly E.B. Morgan's office.

Clockwise from above: Many historic paintings, including this one by nineteenth-century portraitist Charles Loring Elliott, were discovered in Wells College's storage; more of Pleasant's china collection, stored in a cabinet at Leffingwell House; one of many treasures still secreted away in Pleasant's storage barn awaiting the chance to be put on display at one of her inns.

Clockwise from top left: Scenes from Aurora's Main Street: a sign for Aurora Inn, established in 1833; the stately dormer windows and balcony of Zabriskie House; and the bank, built in 1840 by a local stonemason.

Opposite: At Zabriskie House, a pair of parlors is splashed in a custom shade of blue. *Meringue* by Wayne Thiebaud overlooks a chess table.

Above left: In the Zabriskie House dining room, Eric Aho's painting of a chartreuse barn is a perfect match for the striped Clarence House wallpaper.

Above right: Chairs are covered in Galbraith & Paul's handblocked Flora fabric to match. Block paintings by the artist Sam Richardson mirror the color scheme.

Above: Leffingwell House, Pleasant's private home, bears all the hallmarks of her inns, including sentimental touches, like her father's desk and her mother's china.

Opposite: Leffingwell House's breakfast nook is topped with a chandelier from Aurora's MacKenzie-Childs.

Opposite: Rowland House's attic is home to a pair of suites that pay homage to MacKenzie-Childs, the iconic ceramics house Pleasant acquired in 2001. The suites were hand-painted in the brand's classic patterns, Courtly Check and Pure Sunshine. In the black-and-white room, a pair of Chinese folk art paintings add pops of color.

Above: In the yellow suite, Pleasant insisted that the armchair be raised so guests can see the views of Cayuga Lake while seated.

What It's

All For

THE VILLA AT SAUGERTIES

Saugerties, New York

The Villa at Saugerties looks as if it has been standing for at least a century. Its barrel-vaulted roof tiles, its stucco walls, its heavy oak door with a nineteenth-century Spanish knocker. *Who could have built this magnificent manor in modest Saugerties?*, you wonder as you wander beneath billowing weeping willows, amid flowering hydrangea. Perhaps a European duchess who, after coming to New York City, re-created her royal family's country estate away from the public eye?

In truth, The Villa is a little more than a decade old, the artful creation of Amanda Zaslow and Joe Moseley. As effortless as the 3.6-acre estate presents, its four-room inn is nothing short of a dream realized—and what Joe playfully calls "the villa that ten plagues built."

It all started long before they even knew of its existence—on the couple's 2005 honeymoon in Spain. He was a studio manager at Food Network, she an interior designer doing luxury apartments for wealthy Manhattanites. A visit to a quaint inn outside of Barcelona, where the chef-owner served fresh meals from an abundant garden and every day seemed like a magical opportunity to make something beautiful, ignited in them a burning desire to dramatically alter the course of their budding life together. "We had an epiphany," Amanda, who wears her heart on her well-tailored sleeve, remembers. "We thought if we could do something to make people as happy as we felt right then—well, what could possibly be better?"

Amanda Zaslow & Joe Moseley

The honeymoon ended and like many daydreams, the notion simmered on the back burner for years before finally thickening into reality. That fateful day came in 2010 when the pair, burned out from their corporate lives, happened upon the 1920s Mediterranean-style house in the upstate New York hamlet of Saugerties. It had mostly served as a private home, though it operated for a few years as an inn, and a period of abandonment had left it musty and worn. Still, the barn in the back would be perfect for an innkeepers' quarters once renovated, they thought, and the massive pool just needed a few updates and some landscaping. Amanda would handle the design in the main house and its four guest rooms. Joe would put together a menu. They'd be up and running in six months.

Alas, a six-month facelift turned into a six-year epoch of demolition and construction. That funky smell they thought they'd air out in a few days? "Mice—hundreds of them piled up in the walls," Joe recalls with a wince. "They had eaten through most of the electric wiring, so all the walls had to come down and we were forced to vacate to the barn," which was still, at that point, an actual barn with dirt floors. Then came Hurricane Irene. "The barn became Noah's Ark with heavy rains pouring down the walls, frogs coming up through the floorboards, and snakes behind the bed." The storm also ravaged the front yard, which fluctuated between a muddy swamp and, once dried, a dust bowl, necessitating planks as a makeshift pathway. Then, another setback: a new septic system would have to be built. "It was like everything that could go wrong did," Joe says. "Every day was dramatic." And still they persisted. They supervised electric wiring, roofing and tiling, all new plumbing, and the pouring of twelve-inch-thick concrete walls ("I wanted deep window wells," Amanda says, a nod to that old European inspiration). The pool—a forty-foot-long steel drum cut into unforgiving solid ledge—was repaired with new water lines and landscaping. A Venetian plaster expert was brought in. Amanda took on the gardening herself.

Every step was a new skill to throw themselves into and fully master. "We sourced a lot of European fixtures, we wanted classic vaulted ceilings—these were all things the local trade didn't have experience with," Joe says. "Amanda would watch videos and figure out how to make it happen." Meanwhile Joe was on his own R&D mission, poring over notes from his Food Network days, scouting for inspiration from cookbooks, and hounding chef friends and family (and Amanda) for feedback on his latest creations. "He still gets so intense when he's working on a new dish," Amanda says with a laugh. "I learned quickly that I had to be gentle with my feedback!"

It was that good-natured banter—not to mention a lot of tenacity—that somehow saw the duo through it all to New Year's Eve 2016, when, finally, The Villa at Saugerties was born.

Today, organic cotton linens and handmade Moroccan blankets cover the beds in the four guest rooms, and eighteenth- and nineteenth-century antiques sourced from as near as downtown Saugerties and as far as Piedmont, Italy, are placed with meticulous intention on giant wooden armoires and delicate side tables. The reclaimed barn beams crossing the vaulted ceilings are a subtle nod to the rustic origins of Amanda and Joe's own living quarters in the barn—now a minimalist sanctuary just across the gravel drive, next to the natural pond. In the spring, Amanda's gardens burst with clematis, wisteria, and giant purple allium. (In fact, Amanda's gardening habit grew so astoundingly that each guest room has its own outdoor space: a deck with padded loungers just opposite

Page 136: In the dining room, a nineteenth-century Italian walnut buffet and favorite decor pieces sit beneath one of the villa's deep-welled quatrefoil windows.

Previous: The outdoor dining area surrounded by flowering gardens evokes a Mediterranean café with its mosaicked tabletops and striped umbrellas.

Above: In the living room, a nineteenth-century Belgian carved limestone console table is topped with a vintage lamp and antique Antiguan pitcher.

the pool, a picture-book terrace with a mosaicked café table, a secluded garden nestled between a pair of mighty oaks.)

Every morning, Joe makes a three-course breakfast. Sometimes it's shakshuka with garden herbs and local eggs, served with chia seed pudding, fresh blueberries, and pepitas with a dash of spice. Others, it's quinoa-beet cakes topped with sliced avocado, poached eggs, and a parmesan crisp. Always on copious offer are pomegranate cava cocktails and a heavenly muffin of the day.

On many Saturday nights, the couple hosts four-course dinner parties for their guests, where Joe tests out more of his culinary inventions—heavy on vegetables, packed with locally sourced produce, and always creatively seasoned. It is often on these nights, when the couple, crazed and frantic with prepping and hosting and plating and toasting, find themselves most grateful. "One of our first dinners, we were in the kitchen, and Joe was pulling his hair out trying to get everything done just right, and I was racing back and forth making sure everyone was happy," Amanda recalls. "At one point, we were both in the kitchen and we heard the dining room just erupt with laughter. We turned and looked at each other and we both had tears in our eyes. We knew instantly—this moment was the *why*. This was what it was all for. And it was worth it."

Clockwise from above:
The couple built a stylish patio around the existing pool, lining it with double loungers and striped umbrellas; Amanda's gardens reimagined the grounds, with boxwood shrubs, hydrangeas, kousa dogwoods, Japanese maples, clematis vines, and lots of potted annuals and perennials.

Clockwise from bottom left: Joe's muffins of the day are set out on a Moroccan-tiled table for all-day nibbling; the Mediterranean-style stucco villa was rebuilt with twelve-inch insulated block, barrel-vaulted concrete roof tiles, and five chimneys (including one for each guest room); one of Joe's signature breakfasts: crispy quinoa beet cake over a spicy green sauce, with avocado, poached local egg, Parmesan crisp, and La Boite's Peperoncini spice.

Opposite: A guest room's balcony terrace with custom steel railing, eighteenth-century Sicilian lava stone floor, and a mosaicked café table for two.

Above: Joe puts the finishing touches on breakfast at the kitchen's nineteenth-century Dutch walnut table.

Opposite: The guest rooms feature chandeliers made locally and Moroccan wool blankets. The leather-strap headboard was custom-made in Mexico.

Above: In another guest room, a green velvet headboard was made locally. The steel table lamps were custom-made in Mexico.

The Inn-

-tellectuals

THE HENSON

Hensonville, New York

Ely and Danielle Franko didn't dream of an inn. Not at first anyway. She was a dermatology physician assistant—happily—and he was making good money as a software developer at his family's business. There was no burning desire to escape the horrors of the daily corporate slog—nothing like that.

No, it wasn't anything dramatic that prompted the busy Manhattanites to look for a little getaway in upstate New York. "Really, we just wanted a place where we could host dinner parties," Danielle says. Maybe a few weekends a month they'd rent it out for a tidy sum that would cover the mortgage.

In 2016, they found it: a flat-roof A-frame built in the 1970s. It was everything they had hoped for, nestled amid the wild Castkillian forest with a great wall of windows looking out over the trees—though it came with a few less-than-desirable features: water-damaged walls, dated decor that reflected its era with none of the retro nostalgia one might hope for. But that was only half the problem. The other half: "We had no idea how to do a renovation," Danielle says. What they did have was ingenuity—loads of it. Spend enough time with the college sweethearts and you'll get the sense that what drew them together was intellectual curiosity. The two share an almost compulsive willingness to work hard and a strong urge to master new tasks. So they put their clever heads together and, through a trial-and-error education, learned the ins and outs of construction and permitting, drywalling and tiling, painting and spackling, not to mention the less concrete tenets of design like light and space and color and pattern.

Ely & Danielle Franko

It consumed them utterly, occupying their thoughts during the workweek and running them ragged on weekends—still, happily—as they raced from the city to pour every ounce of their collective manpower into their project.

Two years later, the house was done. They threw it up on a few rental sites and prepared to live out their upstate dream. "And within weeks we realized, we're not going to be able to stay here," Danielle said. It blew up. Every night was booked. They had unwittingly created a cash cow. Purchasing another house only made sense, and while they were renovating that house, they came across another listing just down the road and thought, *Why not?* So they bought that and renovated it too, all while still working their city jobs. Oh, and did they mention they got pregnant—twice—in the midst of it all?

By 2021, they were the proud owners of a mini empire of rentals, all of which were so popular that there was hardly a weekend between the three properties for them to enjoy a stay themselves. That's when the idea of an inn finally hit. "Everything had happened so organically up until this point," Ely says. "The momentum just felt right."

They searched and searched, but unlike their house projects, struck out. Then, the old Hensonville Hotel popped up on their radar. Built as a boarding house during the latter half of the nineteenth century, it became an inn sometime in the early 1900s. Though little of its history is known, it was hardly a mystery to Ely and Danielle: during the renovation of their rental properties, Ely had stayed in its modest accommodations more than a dozen times, and let's just say he had not been dazzled. But when it hit the market a few weeks into their search, all memory seemed to have disappeared. Ely could see it: a classic inn, arguably in need of some love, but with great bones and only a stone's throw from the slopes of Windham Mountain. For her part, Danielle couldn't quite bring the vision into focus: "I said, 'Are you insane?'" Between the eye-piercing orange and yellow paint on the walls and the previous owner's predilection for dog memorabilia—statues, stickers, portraits, you name it—the inn's character wasn't immediately evident to her. "But Ely is the dreamer to my realist," she concedes. "He pushes the boundaries of what I think is possible."

They went for it. By now, the couple was living two hours away in Westchester County, and the commute was killing them. Danielle, nearly ready to give birth to their second child, was hardly in any condition for the back-and-forth as it was, and Ely, working his day job remotely, had no need to stay rooted in the suburbs. Thus, on New Year's Day 2021, the family moved into the sixteen-room inn: Ely, Danielle, their three-year-old daughter and three-week-old son, and two dogs—all crammed into rooms 11 and 12.

The couple got to work. Vinyl plastered the floor of every guest room, while original wood floors were almost cruelly doused in layer upon layer of paint. Each ad hoc extension to the building had its own design (or lack thereof), and with it, a litany of era-specific issues. But luck arrived early on when ripping away the vinyl revealed pristine wood floors—different varieties, widths, orientations and finishes, but beautifully intact, nonetheless. They preserved what they could and replaced the rest. The living room was taken down to the studs, ceilings opened up, and skylights installed in what is perhaps one of the best decisions of the entire project: today the room is flooded with a kaleidoscope of natural light that dances across the walls throughout the day.

It was one decision after another, many of which the couple were making for the first time, with nary a formal education in architecture,

INFLATABLE PLANET

Page 152: In the dining room, the artwork is a mix of pieces from Ely's parents' house and paintings collected from 1stDibs, Etsy, and local antique shops.

Previous: All of the wood paneling and banquettes in Matilda were designed by the couple and fabricated out of red oak.

Above: Danielle (here with Ely) learned the art of limewash for the living room. The sofa is Anthropologie; the midcentury table is an Adrian Pearsall design.

Overleaf: The millwork in the library was a late addition that Ely designed with a local artisan. The books became an obsession, arriving in bulk almost by the day.

engineering—not even hospitality! But their type A, methodical approach saved them every time. "It was an iterative process," Ely says, and an exercise in compartmentalization, never thinking too far ahead. "Everything comes down to problems and solutions." Reductive as it sounds, it worked. Ely built what he could himself and hired contractors for the rest, and Danielle mastered all the finish work, teaching herself to limewash, plaster, paint, and stain with medical-grade precision (maybe that physician's assistant background *did* come in handy).

By this point, the couple had established a design sense they were confident in. "In the beginning, we'd buy a bunch of furniture and then return it all because we hated it," Ely says. "Danielle was literally laying tile and then ripping it all up—that happened a few times." Each fail was part of a learning process that over time sculpted a design savoir faire, and it all came to fruition when it was time to furnish The Henson. Ely took the reins in sourcing, scouring sites like 1stDibs and Etsy, as well as Chicago's South Loop Loft. Some items were splurges, like the pair of vintage Tobia Scarpa-style leather armchairs in the living room, while others were carefully executed glow-ups, like the room's minimalist sofa, which the couple reupholstered in a textured gold fabric.

Art and books became an obsession, with boxes arriving daily and by the dozen, containing paintings that spoke to Ely in some way, whether impasto still lifes or antique portraits, and literature and art monographs by the pound, which he carefully sorted marking "keep" or "donate." Above the chess table in the living room, a grouping of remarkable portraits is far more personal, recovered from Ely's late grandparents' home in Turkey and arranged in almost the same gallery layout.

Other pieces came, remarkably, entirely gratis: linens and mattresses from Casper, furniture from Signature Hardware and Arhaus, lighting from Hudson Valley Lighting Group, fixtures from Rejuvenation. How? "It never hurts to ask," Ely says, adding that the collaborations were aided by the large social media following of the couple's rental homes.

While deep in the throes of realizing their inn, Ely dreamed up yet another grand scheme, this time for a restaurant and bar. The couple had long been fans of Contra, the Michelin-starred New York City restaurant owned by restaurateur Fabián von Hauske and chef Jeremiah Stone. What if they approached the partners—who had become friends with the Frankos over the years—to create a new concept? Once again, Ely dared to ask, and once again, the answer was yes.

More than two years after peeling back the first strips of the inn's vinyl flooring, Ely and Danielle cut the ribbon on The Henson. Every corner has been touched personally by the couple. The breathtaking floral arrangements in the entrance? Another skill Danielle picked up. The wooden bar at Matilda, the Contra team's new restaurant? An original inn feature, newly sanded and stained to perfection. The oak bookshelves filled with thousands of lit classics and art tomes? Designed—and filled, book by book—by Ely. And what about the new luncheonette and provisions store down the road? Just a couple of side projects pulled together in their scant free time.

"We just want it all—and we feel capable of doing it all," Ely says. "We like challenges," Danielle echoes. "We like creating things, and we like doing them to the best degree possible." With The Henson anyway, mission accomplished.

franz kafka
JANE AUSTEN

Above: Limited-edition hand-fired tile by Queens, New York–based artisan Helen Levi adds a pop of color to the rustic woodwork in the private dining room.

Opposite: The private dining room centers on a long, early twentieth-century provincial table.

GEORGIA O'KEEFFE
MoMA
The Visual Display of Quantitative Information

Opposite: The lounge at Matilda features an Adrian Pearsall platform sofa that the couple found at Vintage On Point in Los Angeles.

Above: The couple took the formerly dark living room down to the studs, opening up the ceilings, installing skylights, and plastering the fireplace. The Oriolo Rosewood lounge chairs are by Claudio Salocchi.

Clockwise from above:
The couple modernized the classic motel keychain with etched brass; the lamp is called Crinkle by Lyn Godley and Lloyd Schwan, made for the Museum of Modern Art in the 1990s; the couple sourced a variety of vintage objects and books, "the majority center around art exploration and poetry," says Danielle.

Clockwise from above:
Smoked onions with bonito broth at Matilda, named after Ely's grandmother; the French gardens in the backyard are Danielle's latest obsession, the result of months of late-night perennials research; a quaint nook at Day June, the couple's popular-with-the-locals diner down the street from The Henson.

Opposite: The wood banquettes were another custom job designed by the couple and fabricated by local artisans.

Above: The glass bricks between the bar and the dining room are a midcentury nod.

The Long

Way Home

Sullivan County runs through Sims Foster's veins. His family has called the western Catskillian region home for five generations. His parents were schoolteachers in the hamlet of Livingston Manor. His grandfather, a carpenter, built houses in town—many of which still stand—and his great-grandfather ran a bungalow colony on a nearby lake ("Our family's first foray into hospitality," Sims says).

So even when he left Livingston Manor at eighteen, ambitious and ready for a life that would lead him first to West Virginia for college and then to a successful hospitality career in New York City, there was never any notion that Sims had left Sullivan County behind. He ran a small coffee shop in town with his brother, a side hustle that kept him elbow deep in lattes and local gossip whenever he wasn't opening the next hot nightclub or restaurant in Manhattan. And he spoke often, sometimes incessantly, about his home. That was true, and especially impactful, when he met Kirsten Harlow, a senior policy advisor for the Federal Reserve. She found his passion for his hometown endearing—and infectious—and soon, was as smitten with Sullivan County as she was with Sims. As their relationship blossomed, the area played a starring role in every milestone: as the site of weekend trips and family introductions, then the place of their engagement, and finally their wedding.

The wedding, as it turns out, was more than the beginning of a marriage. The couple had invited more than a hundred guests and quickly realized that hotel accommodations in the area were scant. Nevertheless, they cobbled together a beautiful experience for their family and friends—booking a handful in this AirBnB, another dozen in that old inn—and in the process, realized hosting in their beloved second home might be more than a one-time thing. The idea of filling the gap with

Sims Foster & Kirsten Harlow Foster

a hotel of their own wasn't just enticing, it made sense: between Sims's restaurant experience and Kirsten's financial know-how, they were primed to be a hospitality power duo.

Inspired by their Sullivan County love affair, the newlyweds bought Lanza's, an old neighborhood inn with a popular bolt-hole restaurant where Sims had spent many a childhood weeknight with his family. Sims knew the owner well, and the couple had even booked some of their wedding guests there, but they had no illusions about the 1960s-era inn: it needed a lot of work, and it had to be done fast. "A lot of people come into a project like this and take their time for the love of it," says Sims. "Not us—we had a limited budget, and we didn't know if any of this was going to work. We saw it as a litmus test."

They closed on Lanza's in March 2014 and reopened as The Arnold House just two months later, on Memorial Day. They were only nine months married. "It certainly hastened the honeymoon period," Kirsten jokes. And immediately, they took off. Even during the following winter's brutal snowstorms, they maintained a full house.

No sooner had they passed their litmus test than Sims began to think of scaling. Over the next two years, they acquired four more properties, expanding The Arnold House and opening three more inns in Sullivan County, the third of which was an ambitious step into new territory. It was also the inn that would put Foster Supply Hospitality, the couple's newly coined company, on the map.

Called The DeBruce, the old fisherman's lodge wasn't just another inn; it was a physical manifestation of Sims's wildest ideas from his restaurant days. "It was something I had to get out of my system," he says. The rooms were kept spartan and the decor unfussy, while every imaginable detail—and some beyond imagining—was poured into extravagant dinners where each course was more audacious than the last (including an oft-speculated-upon venison dish called the Deer Hang that featured a cured deer's heart hanging on a wire cross). "It was nuts," Sims concedes. But it was another litmus test passed, this one proving that Sullivan County could be a foodie destination—so much so that The DeBruce has been nominated for two James Beard Awards.

By 2016, Sims and Kirsten were full-time Livingston Manorites, and, around town, Sims had become the man to see about an inn. One day, a promising lead came in. Opened in the early 1900s as the Armbrust House, the hilltop inn above picturesque Kenoza Lake was a Victorian dream, with its gabled rooflines, bay windows, and gingerbread trim. The couple was sold from the outset. They signed the deed, then started to strategize what would be their biggest project to date, Kenoza Hall. The boarding house had twenty-nine rooms and just two bathrooms; reconfiguring it for twenty-two en suite rooms was a massive construction feat in and of itself. A dining room was added, and plans for a pool, spa, and ten bungalows on the sprawling parcel behind the house (the property is fifty-five acres in all) were drawn up.

Some of the heaviest lifting, however, came with the design prospectus. Kirsten had slowly "dusted the cobwebs" off her creative right brain for the couple's previous projects, but this was light-years beyond The Arnold House or The DeBruce. Looking to Kenoza Hall's Victorian provenance, the couple put their heads together. Sims drew from his experience creating restaurant concepts, and his years working with major interiors firms like Roman and Williams, while Kirsten embraced new design talents (strengthened by her intense organization and killer ability to put together a spreadsheet). Nearly every detail fell into one of two categories: custom or vintage. For the former, Kirsten collaborated with Castropor, a Portuguese fabricator that built everything, from headboards and side tables to dining tables and chairs, to her specifications. For the latter, the couple scoured antique shops throughout upstate New York

Page 172: Hemlock Neversink's guest rooms are moody and minimal escapes, with custom quilts and Shaker-style woodwork.

Previous: Formerly the Armbrust House, Kenoza Hall dates to the turn of the last century, during a major hospitality boom.

Above: Kirsten and Sims pose with an artwork by Maegan Neubank, a Catskills-based textile artist, at Hemlock Neversink.

Themes emerged, such as cuckoo clocks and what the couple calls their "Kenoza critters," antique figurines of rabbits, birds, and other creatures inspired by the local wildlife bounding around Kenoza Lake. Ever the completist, Sims focused on collecting owls with a near-obsessive enthusiasm. "I cleaned out Newberg. I cleaned out Oswego," he says. "I'd be charging into antique stores asking, *Do you have any owls?!*"

Kenoza Hall opened in 2020, the crown jewel in the couples' expanding portfolio and a significant milestone, elevating them from local innkeepers to influential hoteliers. And still, opportunity continued to knock. Not long after Kenoza was complete, they had already opened the door to their next project: The New Age Health Spa.

Yes, The New Age Health Spa, a prescriptive fortress of 1980s grapefruit-juicing, granola-eating wellness. The 230-acre retreat had long been shuttered. Outdated diet fads and colonic room aside, however, the property was spectacular, all heritage barns and rambling private trails and half-century-old Japanese maples. The usual hurdles were there—infrastructure, septic, electric, design—but by this point, Kirsten and Sims were masters at such things, and renovations came together quickly.

The aesthetic ethos was simpler this time, with subtle nods to the local Quaker culture and farming tradition that would reflect a strong wellness mission. "We wanted to create an aesthetically calming canvas—a neutral palette for whatever journey people need while they're here," Kirsten says. A custom quilt pattern was designed and placed above the spa's barn, like so many historic barns of the area. In the guest rooms, the same pattern was woven onto rugs and blankets, and carved into spindle turned milking stools.

After much deliberation, the couple decided that restoring the solarium pool's *very* vintage design—cheerful chicklet tiles and all—was preferable to ripping it up for some modern marble do-over. "It's got patina," says Kirsten. "It's got personality." The rustic barn at the bottom of the hill is now populated by goats; there's even a goat playground around back, and daily goat hikes are offered. There's also painting and knitting in the art studio, facials and massages in the spa, and just past the plant-forward restaurant, a bonfire overlooking the mountains. They named it Hemlock Neversink, references to the surrounding acres of woods, and the nearby town of Neversink.

A decade after they signed the deed to Lanza's, Sims and Kirsten are no longer newlyweds, neither in the literal sense, nor with regard to their once wide-eyed innkeepers' dream. Altogether, they opened seven hotels, and still found time to have two kids. They sold a few along the way (hotels, that is) and another is in the works—again, a hotel, this one to be set within a trio of historic buildings in nearby Newburgh.

Consequently, they've begun to let go of the little things, hiring others to do what they are now too busy to handle themselves (though never letting go of the insistence that *every single* owl figurine be in the right spot, Sims adds). But their grip on Sullivan County—or rather, its grip on them—has only strengthened: all that it was, all that it is, and now, all that it can be. "It has always been about continuing the special heritage of where I grew up, about being part of rebuilding my hometown," Sims says. "We feel really honored to carry on that tradition."

Previous: The garden patio at Kenoza Hall overlooks Kenoza Lake and the hills of Sullivan County.

Opposite: Sims's fastidious nature is evident in Kenoza Hall's precise placement of books and artwork. In the Rooftop Terrace Suite, vintage landscapes and still lifes are arranged on a gallery wall; books on fishing fill the nearby cabinet.

Above: In the map room, atlases are piled next to the globe. "I can't live in a world where a flower book, which is supposed to be in the fireplace room, is sitting on the table with the maps," Sims says.

Above: The barn quilts of Neversink are a well-known attraction, even earning a scenic tour by a local museum. Kirsten and Sims crafted their own quilt patch for the spa barn at Hemlock Neversink.

Opposite: Hemlock Neversink's airy reception area is filled with designer furnishings and, at its center, a cheeky black sheep sculpture.

COUNTRY PAINTING
PERENNIALS

Opposite and above:
The wood-paneled walls and field-stone fireplace in the lounge at Hemlock Neversink are enhanced with cozy custom sofas and chairs and a collection of antique pottery.

Above and opposite: Kirsten and Sims debated modernizing Hemlock Neversink's indoor swimming pool but instead embraced its retro-chic aesthetic—chicklet tiles included.

Clockwise from above: Hemlock Neversink's goat barn was established with the Frederick Farm Goat Rescue and Sanctuary; the art studio is a place for painting, drawing, knitting, and other creative endeavors; lavender hangs from the outdoor shower in the Hemlock Spa at Kenoza Hall.

BAR

Breakfast
French Omelette 16
grilled toast, bitter greens
Pancakes 15
Sheep's Milk Yogurt 12
rolled oat granola, seasonal fruit
Eggs Any Style 14
grilled toast, bitter greens
Shirred Eggs 17
seasonal vegetable, gruyere
Fruit Plate 10
honey, lemon, poppy seed
Grilled Bacon 12
Breakfast Potatoes 10
Coffee, Tea & Juices
Coffee 4
Espresso 4/6
Apple Cider 5
Orange Juice 5
Grapefruit Juice 5
Cranberry Juice 5
Cold Pressed Juices 12
Green Vitality
kale, cucumber, lemon, celery, fennel, parsley
Pineapple Punch
pineapple, kale, apple
Fresh Start

189

Above left and right: The Trout, sourced from Beaverkill, wrapped in a corn husk, and tied with twine; and The Onion, cooked three ways: salt-baked, sous vide, and pickled.

Opposite: The restaurant at The DeBruce was a chance for Sims to experiment with culinary concepts that had been percolating in his head after decades in the New York City restaurant scene.

The Berkshires

Togethe

THE INN AT KENMORE HALL

Richmond, Massachusetts

It could be argued that style is what led Scott Edward Cole and Frank Muytjens to each other. It was a crisp winter morning. The year: 2016. The setting: the Marlton, Greenwich Village's chic boutique hotel—the kind of place where people don't just pick up their coffee and go, but rather ease into their day.

Frank was ensconced in a sheepskin-upholstered sofa by the fireplace, enjoying a quiet, caffeinated moment before the start of another busy morning running the menswear division of J. Crew. From his cozy perch, he saw Scott. "He was this handsome, manly man, with a beard, and very nicely dressed," Frank recalls.

Scott also noticed Frank, who was no doubt dressed in one of his signature chore coats, his hair tussled as always in its perfectly imperfect coiffure. They struck up a conversation, and realized they had shared interests: Scott, an artist and restaurateur, ran a general store in the Berkshires; Frank had a house about an hour away in upstate New York. They had a few friends in common. And they had the kind of natural ease with each other that felt like kismet. It was the perfect meet cute. "Only after I walked away did I realize, that's Frank Muytjens from J. Crew!" Scott says.

It wasn't long before the two were spending every weekend together in the Berkshires, "religiously," Frank says, living for Friday evenings when they could leave the workweek behind for country things: farmstands, antiques, home-cooked meals.

One night over dinner, early in their relationship, the two realized they had something else in common: Long before they'd met, each had romanticized the idea of owning a bed-and-breakfast. It was a someday dream—if not a someday-soon dream—until a year later, Frank left J. Crew and

Scott Edward Cole & Frank Muytjens

suddenly, the pair found themselves at a crossroads. "We started thinking maybe this idea wasn't that far into the future," Scott says.

Scott, a self-diagnosed "real-estate obsessive," had already been keeping a short list of properties for just such an occasion. At the top of it: a Georgian-Federalist residence built in 1792 by a Revolutionary War soldier. The regal white-columned house sat at a crossroads itself—at the junction of two sleepy farm roads—and its pedigree certainly hinted at greatness. After operating as a boarding school in the 1880s, when it was christened Kenmore Hall, it became a private home and eventually a lodging for musicians and composers in town for Tanglewood, the Berkshires' legendary music venue and festival. It all sounded so bohemian to Scott: creatives performing at all hours of the day and night, pianos in the hallways. Leonard Bernstein even lived in the carriage house for a few years.

But when Scott told Frank about the listing, which had languished on the market for a year, it wasn't exactly music to Frank's ears. "The photos were not impressive at all," Frank says. Still, he agreed to go to a showing the next day. What they found behind the peeling facade was something magical, something just their style: beautiful fireplaces, grand parlors, an elegant Dominican mahogany staircase, all remarkably well preserved. And even further beyond, twenty acres of wooded countryside—a pastoral paradise where they could build a vegetable garden, maybe a flower patch for Frank to plant a few beloved dahlias. "We were blown away," Scott says.

The couple was sold. They'd put in an offer and do a renovation; they'd be open within a year. They'd turn their far-off dream into a present-day reality.

But it wasn't long before they realized the past wasn't quite done with Kenmore Hall. The two-hundred-year-old deed for the land had been split over the ensuing centuries, and the local land court was called in to locate and authenticate a series of ancient documents. It was an archaic process—and painfully slow. "It was almost like dealing with someone with a feather and quill," Scott says. "And there was no way to expedite it."

One month, two months, eventually six months passed. Frank and Scott saw their plans of opening their inn within a year slip away. But there was a silver lining: the sellers gave them carte blanche to access the house, allowing them to bring in contractors and form a plan of action. Even more valuable, it gave them quiet moments to deeply consider what to do with the place. "Sometimes we would just sit in a room and say, 'What is this room asking for?'" Franks says.

By the first snowfall, Kenmore Hall was officially theirs, and July 1, their target opening date, was a mere six months away. Luckily, the bones were in good shape. "The moldings and millwork were all intact," Scott says. "Unlike so many historic buildings, this one hadn't been bastardized terribly over the years." The slate roof and chimney tops needed repairs, the kitchen needed a full gut, and the electric and heating systems needed replacing—but the rest of their work would be largely cosmetic.

They dove in. Up to forty workers crowded in every day, different crews working side by side, laying new pipes, building new floors, and carving closets and bathrooms out of old passageways that ran the perimeter of the house. The blush pink carpet in the foyer was pulled up to reveal beautiful wood flooring, which the couple had stained the old-fashioned way, with an apple cider vinegar solution. "If you put a rusty nail in it, it corrodes and creates a natural stain," Scott says. "It was just the right dark patina."

Frank and Scott rolled up their sleeves too, dutifully fulfilling tasks assigned to them by their contractor: scraping wallpaper, painting walls. It was during these phases of the renovation that the couple's styles converged to make magic. "We don't have exactly the same tastes, but they are

EVIDENCE
1944 1994
RICHARD
AVEDON

Page 194: The white-columned entry of Kenmore Hall, a Georgian-Federalist residence built in 1792 by a Revolutionary War soldier.

Previous: Room Two's velvet sofa is topped with pillows hand-sewn by Frank using fabric from his extensive textile collection.

Above: Daisies and branches of a crabapple tree climb a brick wall in the backyard. An orchard with century-old heirloom apple, pear, and cherry trees lies just beyond.

complementary," Scott says, and even when their design sensibilities were at odds, they always seemed to naturally meet in the middle. Ultimately, the couple decided on a masculine palette—a nod to Frank's career in menswear and an homage to the Hancock Shaker Village three miles from the inn.

Furniture was as much a blending of styles as a blending of possessions. There was plenty to combine between Scott's house in the Berkshires and Frank's New York City apartment and Hillsdale home—all of which they gave up for Kenmore Hall. What they didn't already have, they shopped for, in antique stores and estate sales from Chatham to Hudson, at the Brimfield Flea Market in central Massachusetts, and at showrooms in the city. It all came together seamlessly, even, at times, in the unlikeliest combinations, such as in the front parlor, where a honey-colored antique wood table is a perfect match for Frank's beloved Paul McCobb chairs. The layering of old and new has a collected-over-time feeling that's not about perfection or curation so much as character.

They finished on time—early, actually—opening their newly rechristened Inn at Kenmore Hall in late June. Immediately they fell into their new roles, which, true to form, were complementary. Scott makes breakfast, of course, and Frank works the front-of-house of the casual dining room, delivering his partner's made-to-order eggs and omelets with local apple-cider doughnuts and piping hot coffee. (In reality, there is little to distinguish the front of the house from the back; even the kitchen is beautifully designed, and guests often wander in from the terraces by the lawn.) "We really want people to feel as though they are guests in someone's home," Scott says.

And it is their home: The couple lives in an apartment above the kitchen. It is their collection of books and magazines (about everything from Brancusi to Balenciaga) on the coffee tables; their boombox and cassette tapes (Bjork and Bow Wow Wow) in the back parlor; their personal art collection on the walls (including the first painting Scott ever bought, hung over the bar cart). The pillows on the sofas aren't just theirs—they are Frank's creations, sewed from his extensive collection of textiles. Their work boots and wellies are even set out by the front door, a laidback welcome to all who enter, and encouragement to kick off your own shoes and get comfy.

These days, the inn is like a well-oiled machine, leaving the couple ample time to work on their next project: Kenmore Hall's gardens. It's a passion they fuss over with great care and patience—the bright herbs, the climbing crabapple trees, the fat, juicy tomatoes. But nothing quite compares to the dahlias, rows upon rows of carefully nurtured cultivars: peachy, bulbous Orange Globes; raspberry-colored KA's Rosie Jos; and dazzling coral and pink Labyrinths. "Scott likes to joke that I know the names of these dahlias better than I do the names of some of his friends," Frank says, laughing.

Should you happen upon the two of them in the gardens, happily pruning and potting, you'll see for yourself the natural ease that Scott and Frank share, as individuals, as a couple, and as stewards of their inn. They work quietly and happily, they do not rush but rather relish in their task, and they take pride in all they have created. That comfort seems to have rubbed off on The Inn at Kenmore Hall, and in turn, as if by osmosis, it washes over their guests. And they know it too: "It's work that we really, really love to do," Scott says. "We pinch ourselves every day that we find ourselves lucky enough to do it."

Clockwise from above: Tomes of the couple's favorites artists, architects, and designers populate the coffee table in the back parlor; personal objects—combined when Frank and Scott sold their respective homes from New York City to Monterey, Massachusetts—give the inn a lived-in feel. "We do live here, so everything is exactly how we like it," Scott says; some of the couple's favorite books and objects are on display in the back parlor.

The garden is where Frank and Scott spend most of their free time, nurturing their beloved dahlias, as well as tomatoes, radishes, kale, and other produce that gets used in the kitchen.

Above left and right: In Room Three's bathroom, the floor had to be reinforced to support a giant soaking tub. The walls were painted a nearly black hue to match the marble fireplace.

Opposite: A gilded stool and vintage standing mirror add a touch of glam.

CHICAGO PUBLIC LIBRARY
JOY OF GARDENING
ENGLISH GARDENS
MODERN

Opposite: The couple, on a break from tending to their dahlias.

Above: The garden cottage is a place for learning and daydreaming: quilts and cozy pillows are stacked on the daybed, and gardening books are piled high on the center table, along with packets of seeds and farm tools.

# of Yes

Twenty-five years ago, a boy named Terry met a girl named Terri. The place was Gramercy Tavern, the iconic New York City restaurant. Terry, a recent theater graduate from California State University, was working as a waiter, and Terri, a model from Texas by way of Miami, was the restaurant's new maître d'. There was a first date, and on that first date a question: "What is your ultimate dream in life?" Terry asked. "One day, I want to run a bed-and-breakfast," Terri replied. "Yes, me too!" Terry responded without hesitation. In fact, innkeeping had never crossed Terry's mind—until this five-foot-ten vision with twinkling blue eyes and a laugh that possessed her entire body had said it. "I was just super madly in love," he says.

They were engaged three months later—but the inn did not come just yet. Terry rose through the ranks, becoming a right-hand man to celebrity restaurateur Danny Meyer, managing this restaurant, opening that one, until twenty years later he was Union Square Hospitality Group's director of operations. By then, Terri was a stay-at-home mom, raising the couple's children, Ro and Grace, and Terry, effectively running an empire, was working long, often late, hours. "Like so many people who study acting, I got into hospitality because I loved the production of it all—the performance, the energy, the human connection," he says. "But the higher up I got, the more removed I became from that thing I originally loved."

Terri & Terry Coughlin

So the couple went away—not far—just a few hours away to the Berkshires. It was a celebration of sorts: twenty years to the day of that first date. They checked into the charming five-room Inn at Kenmore Hall and spent the weekend sleeping on crisp linen sheets and soaking in their suite's claw-foot tub. They talked about that first date. They talked about the ultimate dream. "Suddenly, it lit us up," Terri says.

The following week went something like The Cure's *Friday I'm in Love*: "We came home on a Sunday," Terri recalls. "Monday, I ordered the same linen sheets they have at Kenmore. Wednesday we were really talking about it, and by Friday it was like, *What are we waiting for?* The following Saturday, we were looking at a property." It didn't even feel like a decision. The answer was yes. They bought it.

And just like that, they were innkeepers-in-the-making. Terry gave his notice. The family moved into the rear wing of the house. The Terries set to work. The white-columned mansion on the corner of Division Street and North Plain Road in Great Barrington had a long and stately history, built in 1825 and expanded into a grand estate by its second owner, John Henry Coffing, best known in history as one of the delegates who nominated Abraham Lincoln for the presidency during the 1860 Republican National Convention. The property had changed hands remarkably few times in its two centuries, such that when the Terries first stepped foot inside, they discovered beautiful hardwood floors, decorative moldings, and a well-preserved double-sided fireplace on the first floor. Upstairs, however, left far more to be desired: having operated at some point as a bed-and-breakfast (or, perhaps more accurately, a flophouse) it was a jumbled grid of modest bedrooms and shared bathrooms. The couple envisioned a new floorplan of five unique guest rooms—two of them larger suites—with living rooms and lounges for guests downstairs.

Though Terry especially had plenty of experience in cultivating a hospitable environment in trendy restaurants where stars and celebrities were regular fixtures, creating—and more importantly, budgeting—an entire inn was new territory altogether. "I was wickedly off the mark on a few things," he recalls. "Roads and framing blew our budget." But where finances were tight, ingenuity and personality made up the difference, with the couple splashing every space with their own personal effects, along with a high-low blend of design pieces: Scandinavian furniture and vintage trunks, art and books collected over the couple's lives, and plenty of nostalgic touches, such as a framed ticket to the top of the Empire State Building (where Terry proposed) and a Mercedes hubcap on one wall saved from the 1970 Benz that Terry bought for Terri as a wedding gift. ("It was only $1,000, and it was wrecked within the year," Terry says with a laugh.)

"We wanted everything to connect—to the history of the house, to our Berkshires setting, and to us and our family," Terry says. In the dining room, the walls and ceiling beams were painted a dark blue-green, an homage to the dining room at Union Square Cafe. (The paint color's fitting name? Tarrytown.) In the yard, Terri nursed the roots of century-old peony bushes back to life and turned a tiny shed overlooking Monument Mountain—where legend has it, Nathaniel Hawthorne once encouraged Herman Melville to write *Moby Dick*—into a cozy reading room for one. On the walls throughout the mansion, historic documents, portraits of long-lost strangers (and a few of Abraham Lincoln) were hung. And in the small alcove near the billiard table, Terry created a listening room, displaying his extensive collection of vinyl, from

Page 212: "Start with yes" is an old hospitality adage . . . and a reminder of Terry and Terri's first date, when they agreed to a mutual dream of opening an inn.

Previous: The backyard's tiny shed was converted into a reading room for one. "The previous owner hosted intimate tea parties in it," Terri says.

Above: The Greek Revival home was built in 1825. Its stately Doric columns and classical pediment are original designs.

Overleaf: In the living room a vintage metal cabinet is a place for guests to put their feet up. The armchair is in the style of Hans Wegner's Papa Bear lounge.

Elvis Presley and the Beastie Boys to Dolly Parton and Berkshires icon James Taylor, along with a guitar and a cozy sofa.

A year after buying the mansion, the Terries put the final touches on their inn: over the fireplace, a painting by Robert Kushner, a gift from Danny Meyer; and above the glowing jukebox, a sign that reads, in bold red letters, START WITH YES. It's an old hospitality adage—"Even when the answer is no, you find some way to make the customer happy," Terry says—but it's also a reminder of that first date, when Terri divulged her ultimate dream and her smitten suitor emphatically agreed to it, no questions asked.

They christened their dream realized Granville House, named after—what else?—the Old Granville House from *It's a Wonderful Life*. And a wonderful life it is. Every morning, Terry makes breakfast to order, always accompanied by his now-famous olive-oil muffins, a recipe borrowed from one of his former pastry chefs at Union Square Hospitality Group. Terri tends to the growing gardens and together the couple perfects the mise-en-scène, as they put it. "Every day is like curtain-up," Terry says. "Everything on set has to be perfect—the music has to be perfect, the lighting has to be perfect. It scratches that creative actor's itch for me."

And with each new cast of characters that arrives, the couple starts with yes, welcoming them into their thoughtfully curated home like old friends. There is no greater pleasure than finding that a guest has scrapped their plans for the day to cozy up with a book or a game on the sunlit porch or dig through the record collection for old classics and new favorites. (All the guest rooms also have their own record players—there's even one in the bathroom in Room Five—and the Terries encourage guests to borrow as many albums as they like. "We had a very quiet older couple stay with us once, and after they checked out, we found Meatloaf, Led Zeppelin—all this '70s rock—in their room," Terri recalls. "We loved getting to see that little hidden side of them.")

And every now and then, it hits them: "We get to create this perfect little production and live in this historic 1825 mansion—which otherwise we could never afford—and people actually pay us to be a part of it," Terry says. "And because of that we don't have to get real jobs." Who could say no to that?

The Essential Cy Twombly
Andy Warhol—From A to B and Back A

THE BERKSHIRES
WES ANDERSON

Clockwise from above: Terry's now-famous morning muffins are a recipe borrowed by one of the Union Square Hospitality Group's pastry chefs; the dining room is an homage to Terry's long career at the group: the walls are painted the same color as Gramercy Tavern's private dining room; Terry and Terri on the front steps of the inn.

Top left and above: The listening room is an homage to the couple's favorite musicians, from Beethoven to the Beastie Boys. Every room at the inn has its own record player, and guests are encouraged to borrow albums for private listening. Bottom left: The table in the inn's entry is piled with country antiques, potted plants, and birds' nests.

Opposite: Room Three's bay window seat is topped with Swiss Army pillows by BOBO. The midcentury modern–style molded plywood rocking chairs are from One Forty Three.

Above: *James Stewart #2* by Peter Stackpole is framed over the bed in Room Four. "I've been obsessed with Jimmy Stewart since I was nineteen," Terry says. The blanket is Pendleton's Yakima Camp Throw.

Vermont

The Manor

Reborn

THE INN AT BURKLYN

East Burke, Vermont

The first time Marci and Jim Crone saw Burklyn Hall, it was via text. "I found your house," the message read, along with a picture of a stately Colonial Revival mansion perched atop a rolling Vermont hill.

It was a recurring joke between Marci and her cousin, with whom she had grown up on the East Coast. Marci had since found her way to California, where she and Jim had it all: a successful commercial real estate business, five children, six grandchildren, and a beautiful home where the family gathered at least once a week for big dinners or barbecues. Still, Marci had always fantasized about a return to her native coast.

She showed the listing to Jim. "It's pretty," he agreed. "But I'm not moving to Vermont." Anyway, they agreed, a thirty-five-room house on eighty-six acres was too much house for them.

And that was that. Or so Marci thought.

Two weeks later, Jim called her from work. "He told me to pack for the weekend—we were getting on a plane," she recalls. "I said, 'I'm going to need more information than that.'" Jim invited her to his office, where a photo of Burklyn was displayed on a big presentation screen. "I bought it!" he said. "We're going out there this weekend to see it." It was all so romantic.

Well, says Jim, it wasn't *only* romance that inspired the sudden change of heart. "It was a tax exchange," he explains, referencing an IRS rule that allows investors to forgo capital gains payments when they apply the profits from one property to the purchase of another. Jim had recently sold a building and needed to quickly channel the proceeds into a new venture. Marci's fateful text had arrived at just the right time.

Marci, Jim & Michael Crone

Never mind the business details, Burklyn was theirs if they wanted it. They had ten days to sign the paperwork or back out of the deal. So they hopped on the next flight to Burlington and drove the two hours through rambling farmland, past glassy lakes and boreal forests, to the great house on the hill.

It had been built in 1908 by Elmer Darling, a local aristocrat who made his fortune operating New York City's Fifth Avenue Hotel ("the Plaza of the time," says Marci). As one of Vermont's most prominent citizens, he was integral to bringing the area its first hydroelectric power plant. In his Vermont home, he had duplicated many of his enterprises' luxuries and innovations, including an elevator (one of the state's first) and a high-tech power grid that operated on both gas and new-fangled electric. Ornate details were in abundance as well: rich mahogany paneling and hand-carved wood accents, custom crystal sconces and extravagant plaster moldings, and ten marble fireplaces—one even crowned with the Darling family's crest.

When Marci and Jim first laid eyes on Burklyn, it was every bit the noble manse they had imagined, save for some rough edges, such as the porch ("falling in," says Marci) and the paint (a medley of every hue of yellow). Inside, they found that the grand staircase was missing more than a few balusters, and at least half of the eighteen bedrooms appeared to have been left empty and collecting dust for years. But even through the disrepair and dated decor, the couple could see Elmer Darling's creation for what it was: "Too beautiful to let go of," says Marci.

Still, it *was* too much house for just the two of them. That night, Jim stayed up late devising a plan that would enable them to keep it, and come morning, he had the answer: Burklyn Hall might not make financial sense, but The Inn at Burklyn? That just might work. Marci and Jim would relocate to Vermont, renovate the estate, and once completed, hire an innkeeper to run the place. "We saw it as a retirement project," Jim says. "I was going to have fun doing all the moldings and the woodwork. Marci was going to give the entire place her designer's touch. And then we'd go back to California and have a nice passive income."

Renovations began in earnest. First things first, Jim brought in an electrician and a plumber. The latter was immediately confronted with a bigger-than-expected project when the fire marshal informed Jim that every lead-soldered copper pipe—that is, every single pipe in the house—would need to be replaced. Walls and floors were carefully opened and resealed, a monumental (not to mention, expensive) process made bearable only by the discovery that the house's electric was blissfully up to code.

While he was no rookie in matters of construction, Jim soon realized that restoring an early 1900s landmark was a far cry from the office buildings and shopping centers he'd built in the past. "There was no going to Home Depot with this project," he says. "I needed to make everything look like it was built in 1908." To do that, he set up a wood shop in the basement and replicated moldings, balusters, and other ornate details with a commercial-grade router.

While Jim was elbow-deep in sawdust, Marci was making herself a regular fixture at the local community center, where she unearthed books, correspondence, and artifacts from Elmer Darling himself. What she learned of Burklyn Hall's creator impressed her so much, it ultimately informed her entire design concept. "I realized how much thought he put into this home, and felt I had no choice but to honor it." But honoring didn't mean replicating. In fact, to truly do Burklyn justice, Marci believed evolution was in order. "Elmer Darling was an innovator, and he would have wanted to keep up with the times, so while I wanted to make his home beautiful again, it had to be current and relevant to today."

Archival photographs served as guides for her updated design schemes. In the formal dining room, originally painted blue, she lined the walls

Page 226: The fireplace in the main entry bears the Darling coat of arms. A pair of beaded sconces are believed to have been custom designed by Elmer himself.

Previous: Views over the Vermont countryside from the antique window at the top of the grand staircase.

Above: Archival photographs showed the dining room painted a royal blue. Marci honored that palette with Pyne Hollyhock floral wallpaper from Schumacher.

with blue floral wallpaper from Schumacher and filled the mahogany cabinets with delft china. In the walk-in safe, still filled with Darling's documents and personal correspondence, she unearthed old wallpaper—two whole rolls of it—and, through photos, determined it had once lined the walls of the Egypt Suite (named for its views of the nearby area known as Little Egypt). Six long panels were framed and placed on the walls of the suite, which she rechristened its original name with a bronze plaque on the door.

Altogether, the renovations took two years—"and every day there was an *oh shit* moment," Jim laughs—but at last, they completed their marvelous manor. The new innkeeper moved into the apartment in the back of the house, ready to take on her role. The first guests arrived that autumn, just as the driveway pavement was drying. Marci and Jim returned to their lives in California.

And that was that. Or so they thought.

Six months later, Marci received a call from the innkeeper. "She didn't like it—it was too much work," she recalls. She was throwing in the towel. "She gave us nine days' notice."

For the second time, Jim and Marci raced across the country to save Burklyn. Only this time, there was no choice in it: "We had to take over," Marci says. "It couldn't stop. There were reservations, events. There was no hitting the pause button."

As adept as the couple were at making a beautiful inn, they had almost zero experience in hospitality. "I was a busboy in Caesar's Palace when I was sixteen," Jim says, with a laugh. No time to lament, they dove in head-first. Marci, an excellent home cook, expanded the breakfast menus, and even started opening the dining room for dinner. Their kids got involved too: Madison managed the housekeeping team and worked in the restaurant. Jaya took over as events manager and, working with Hilary, still back in California, ran social media accounts. And Michael, the middle son, who had been working for years in the family real estate business, came on as the second-generation innkeeper.

The group effort freed Marci and Jim to consider what else they might do with Burklyn. They hired a professional chef and opened the dining room to the public, first with a series of popular pop-ups and eventually as a full-time restaurant. Jim, an oenophile, crafted an impressive wine list. Meanwhile, Michael realized he had a talent for hospitality and the gift of gab. "I tell the staff to come grab me if I am talking to someone for more than five minutes, because otherwise I will chat with the guests all night," he says.

Michael's gusto for the innkeeping life has finally allowed Marci and Jim their retirement. Well, call it semiretirement. Many evenings you'll find them passing through the parlor, saying hello to guests, checking in on the kitchen staff, reviewing the reservations for the week. Innkeeping may have never been on their life list—not even after they bought Burklyn—and yet somehow, they've comfortably landed right in the midst of it. Often, they'll make like guests themselves, walking through the gardens and the apple orchard or sipping a glass of wine on the porch and watching the painterly views over Lake Willoughby Gap. In these moments, all the hard work doesn't just feel worth it—it feels like the making of their golden years. "In a lot of ways, it's hard to believe we're here, that we achieved all of this, especially during this time of our life," Marci says. "But it's been one of the most rewarding experiences of our life—and a true honor."

Above left: The expansive grounds include two orchards and several gardens with sculptural topiaries and burbling fountains.

Above right: When Marci and Jim first saw the mansion, its exterior was every hue of yellow, "like the previous owners just touched it up with whatever they could find," says Jim. The couple painted it to match archival photographs of the estate.

Opposite: Painterly views over East Burke from the inn's second floor.

Opposite: Marci decorated the library as she imagined Elmer Darling would have used it, with a handsome velvet blue sofa and areas for reading and playing chess.

Above: The light fixture in the library is believed to be Tiffany; its silk top has long since disintegrated, and what is left of its fringe is uneven, but Marci considers it a treasure no less.

Above: In the Brighton Suite, Versailles wallpaper and matching fabric is from Schumacher.

Opposite: Artist G. Bourne's painting of a barn hangs over the marble fireplace in Brighton.

IAN McEWAN SWEET TOOTH

Clockwise from above: Historic photographs of Burklyn during construction and floorplan drawings were discovered in the walk-in safe on the first floor of the house; keys hang in the inn's reception; an original transom operator (sadly decommissioned for fire safety) and still-operating push-button switch in Brighton.

Clockwise from top left: Jim carefully matched and re-created staircase balusters and other wood details using a commercial-grade router in the basement; Jim, Michael, and Marci on the inn's grand wraparound porch; fluffy chocolate muffins served on delicate china for breakfast.

Little Inn,

Big Family

EDSON HILL

Stowe, Vermont

The first time Susan Stacy laid eyes on Edson Hill, it was one of those picture-perfect Vermont winter nights: brisk and quiet, snowflakes gently fluttering from a blackened sky, blanketing the earth in a soft coat of shimmering white. The barn was shuttered; from inside, an occasional horse's neigh cut through the silence. Across the valley, beyond the frozen lake, the brick manor house was still, mounds of fluffy snow collecting on its steep sloping roof, dormer windows lit by a warm glow. "I play that night back in my head often," Susan says. "The moment we drove up the driveway, my mind started wandering. I kept asking myself, *What could this be*?"

The question lingered long enough for Susan and her husband, Tom, on one of their annual ski trips to Stowe, to return to Edson Hill several more times that weekend. The couple had learned of the inn on a lark, while flipping through a real estate circular at their regular après-ski bar. Susan, an interior designer based in Cape Cod, had done projects in the area—including a residence less than a mile from Edson Hill—but she had never seen, nor even heard about, this idyllic retreat.

Still, for more than half a century it had operated as an inn—and, for the better part of that time, a wildly popular one at that. The manor house, originally built as a private estate in 1940 by a wealthy gold prospector from Rhode Island, opened as an exclusive guesthouse in 1951, just as Vermont's ski scene entered its heydey. Surrounded by Nordic trails, it was the site of countless parties drawing an upper-crust clientele. In the ensuing years, the

The Stacy Family

inn changed hands several times, parceling out the original 550-acre estate and adding a handful of slope-roofed outbuildings along the way.

The next winter, back in Stowe for another ski season, Susan and Tom returned for another look at the old inn, still on the market. A year of renovation ideas had been percolating. "I already had the whole thing designed in my head," Susan says. It was time to ask the questions aloud. "We were skiing with my brothers-in-law, who are in finance and real estate development, and I posed it to them: What would it take?" Numbers were crunched, calls were made, and soon, papers were signed. The family was all in: Susan would design. Tom and the brothers would manage the finances. "They gave me a budget and a deadline, and I was off and running," she says.

There was much work to be done: All the decor was thrown out, and the foyer was modified for a more welcoming arrival. The small pub in the basement was especially in need of a makeover. "It felt like a Howard Johnson's banquet hall," Susan recalls. "There was Astro turf on the floor and maybe four laminate tables—very bleak!" But little discoveries awaited: delft tiles depicting countryside scenes surrounded the fireplace in the great room, for instance, and the manor's original wood beams—salvaged from the homestead of Revolutionary War hero and founding Vermont statesman Ethan Allen—were bright spots amid the dark, frilly, outdated design.

Susan enlisted the team at her Boston interiors firm, all of whom were eager to tackle a dream project (the kind *without* a client, Susan says with a laugh). The driving aesthetic would be, simply, to feel like a home—"not some corporate hotel." Each of the twenty-two rooms would have its own personality, with plenty a nod to the Vermont setting: vintage ski posters and antique snowshoes on the walls, four-poster beds and cozy sofas piled high with earth-toned blankets and pillows, and deep soaking tubs that would look out onto the surrounding forest.

For the manor house's public areas—the great room with the roaring fireplace, the dining room, and the downstairs tavern—Susan called on some of her favorite fabricators and makers for custom jobs, then augmented the spaces with antiques and art from auction houses and local dealers like Vermont's Hogback and Buggy Man Antiques. "I wanted everything to be found and not hugely recognizable," she says. The project was finished in six months—and nearly on budget, a feat Susan happily reflects on. "It was all-hands-on-deck and lots of late nights, but everyone was working with a smile on their face. I would do it a million times over again."

Edson Hill's transformation may have been complete, but this was hardly the inn's last chapter. The family's financial geniuses had made the deal happen, and its design ace had ushered in a dazzling new vision, but who would take the reins from there was another question. The answer awaited, perhaps unsurprisingly, within the family: Susan's brother Erik Stacy. While Susan had always been the family's artist, Erik was its adventurer, an accomplished sailor and skier whose sporting style had taken him to the British Virgin Islands to work in sales at a resort. He had watched from afar as his sister threw herself into her Vermont passion project—and, later, as the inn cycled through two general managers in less than two years. Having just returned to the US with his wife, Jesse, and the couple's two daughters, he was pondering his next move. Susan was hardly subtle when she approached the couple to join the inn, not just as managers, but as partners. "I know it can be scary to work with family," she says, "but I knew they were perfect for the job."

Page 242: The inn's lounge is a place to gather by a fire, among antiques and original artworks sourced by interior designer and co-owner Susan Stacy.

Previous: A horse grazes in the snow at the inn's barn by the lake.

Above: Jesse and Erik in the tavern, which Susan updated with leather banquettes, reclaimed wood beams, and archival photographs from Stowe's heyday.

And so, the Edson Hill family expanded—and so did Edson Hill. Ever on a quest for an epic adventure, Erik assumed the sizable task of reviving the thirty-eight-acre estate's backcountry trails, establishing a private network of routes for cross-country skiing and snowshoeing, and building a Nordic center with gear from French alpine ski outfitter Rossignol. Meanwhile, Jesse elevated the inn's day-to-day operations, expanding its culinary program and augmenting Susan's design vision, even adding her own touch with a handful of delicate paintings, which now hang in the great room. The vital final pieces of the Edson Hill puzzle, Erik, Jesse, and their daughters slowly built the heart and soul of the inn over the next several years, living on the grounds of the estate—both a blessing and a curse, to hear the couple tell it. "There were no days off," Erik says. "But that's part of the appeal: our girls have grown up here, and people are drawn to the fact that we're a real family—it's all very authentic and it's what makes this feel like home for our guests."

These days, Edson Hill is enjoying its second heyday. Even on a Tuesday night, the dining room is abuzz, with hearty dishes like local venison rack and berbere-spiced lamb flying out of the kitchen to diners gathered around a lively communal table beneath a chandelier of tangled tree branches. The tavern, mercifully relieved of its artificial grass, brims with activity too, with patrons tucking into gourmet burgers at leather banquettes and the carved wooden bar (where you'll often find Jesse pouring wine, or Erik throwing back a beer with a local). And in the great room, nothing fills Jesse with more pride than the sight of guests lingering for one more nightcap, their eyes dancing with the glow of the delft-tile lined fireplace. It's a home made from a collective vision and a group effort, existing only by the combined energy of its cast of patrons, each committing their own artistry, passion, and elbow grease to a greater cause. "There's just a lot of love here," Jesse says. "There's so much care and pride and hard work that has gone into this place. It just warms my heart."

Previous: "I wanted it all to feel slightly worn—not precious—timeless but also clean," Susan says. Dark wood paneling, four-poster beds, and deep soaking tubs achieve the look in the guest rooms.

Above and opposite: The rustic charms of Edson Hill: piles of firewood stacked at the ready to warm the winter nights, Nordic trails for snowshoeing and cross-country skiing, and a wooden toboggan in the barn.

Top right: Susan's tree-branch chandelier in the restaurant was a clever—and cost-free—creation: "We ventured into the woods and foraged for it," she says. "This April we'll go back out and make another one." Above, bottom right, and opposite bottom: Meals at the Edson Hill restaurant are rustic and hearty: poached eggs served in a skillet, roasted salmon on a bed of winter vegetables, and bone-in ribeye steak with savory tomato stew.

Above: Fresh snow gathers on the pitched roof on a crisp wintery morning.

Opposite: In the lounge, Susan hung a painting by Sarah Hinckley, an artist who once lived in the Cape Cod home the interior designer resides in today. "It was serendipitous moments like that that made me think this all was meant to be."

Above left: The delft tiles surrounding the fireplace are original to the 1940 estate.

Above right: Overstuffed sofas and armchairs were custom upholstered.

Maine

Kings of

the Castle

THE NORUMBEGA INN

Camden, Maine

Inns are a dime a dozen in Maine. But a castle? Well, that's something.

Architect Will Tims and his partner, Brett Haynie, knew it was something from the moment they first saw it: Norumbega Castle, an 1886 manor set on a rolling hill, a mere stone's throw from the Camden Harbor. It had been built by Joseph Barker Stearns, the inventor of the duplex telegraph, who was enlisted by Western Union to take his newfangled technology to Europe. There, he went from country to country selling his communication system and, during his time off, visited the great estates of the continent: Versailles, Buckingham, Balmoral.

When he returned home to Maine a newly minted millionaire, he was moved to build a castle that would be the envy of all. It would be replete with its own royal trappings, from fieldstone walls and golden oak paneling to stained-glass windows and a splendid tower topped with an even more splendid turret, positioned to enjoy views over Penobscot Bay and its Lilliputian islands. He filled his Shangri-La with his favorite possessions: his library of ten thousand books, his collection of Chiriquí pottery, his Queen Anne antiques. He named it Norumbega, after the fabled golden city mythologized by French explorers who settled the Northeast during the 1600s. They reported a resplendent place, with palaces of gold and women wearing quarts of pearls about their heads. This fantasyland, of course, never existed, but in his castle, Stearns had made it real.

A century and a half later, Will and Brett turned down Norumbega's porte cochere and

Brett Haynie & Will Tims

waltzed (one must always waltz here) through its still-very-grand entrance. Technically they were guests—the castle had operated as an eleven-room guesthouse over the preceding decades—but like the sixteenth-century settlers seeking the lost city of Norumbega, they were on their own reconnaissance mission: for an inn project.

Will and Brett were the only guests that wintery evening, the first of four nights they had planned to spend touring inns across Maine. On the market for two years, Norumbega had danced through their dreams ever since they saw its real estate listing, but the castle's scale and grandeur were intimidating. All hesitation disappeared the minute they walked through the door. They were spellbound. "There was a crazy storm that night," Brett recalls, "and the owners basically gave us the keys and left us in the castle by ourselves." The couple opened a bottle of wine and wandered about, peeking into every room, and envisioning what they might do with each space. "I remember saying to Will, 'Even if we don't buy this property, this was such a magical night,'" Brett says.

What they found behind each door was inspiration: Stearns's two-story library (empty but still impressive), original clawfoot tubs. The woodwork alone was a sight to behold. And even in the midst of a furious storm, the expansive grounds were undeniably swoon-worthy, with a romantic gazebo designed to match the main house. When the sun came up the next morning, the storm had passed—but none of the sorcery of the previous night had worn off. This was their magic castle. Though they went on to tour the remaining seven inns on their itinerary, their search was already over.

The couple had been circling the idea of an inn for a few years. Will, an architect working as a design director for a major real estate developer, had overseen a number of large hospitality projects. It was intense work, and not always fulfilling. "I was feeling overworked and burned out," he recalls. "More and more, I felt an urge to change my life and do something that felt more satisfying."

An inn was a natural pivot, a chance to build on his knowledge of the hotel business—on his own creative terms. The idea lingered for years before morphing into something resembling a dream. "It wasn't like this was a lifelong aspiration," Will says. Meanwhile, Brett was in the midst of his own transition—realizing his aspirations of being an opera singer. "Every door I knocked on seemed to be opening," he says. A move to the stages of Paris seemed imminent.

When Will brought up the subject of an inn, Brett was supportive, if not quite ready to roll up his sleeves and pitch in. "I was very much in opera land," Brett recalls with characteristic panache. It was too early to say exactly what would happen. They'd keep their apartment in the city, where Brett would continue to work with his voice coaches while Will searched for the right property. They'd figure the rest out as it came.

Their first days at the castle were steady as she goes, though the couple felt more like serfs than kings. The inn came as is—dated furniture and all—and rather than make any hasty business decisions, they decided to operate it in its current condition for a full season. They moved into the innkeeper's apartment downstairs. Will ran the day-to-day, while Brett commuted weekly back to the city for voice lessons and rehearsals. Together, during their evenings and moments of free time, they designed the future of their little kingdom.

The following winter, they closed the inn and prepared to renovate. Nearly every inch of the 140-year-old golden oak panels, wainscotting, coffers, shelves, and moldings were immaculate, blessedly never painted. The house's nine fireplaces were remarkably pristine, this one with ornate sculptural

Page 258: The drawing room's matching L-shaped sofas are from Mitchell Gold. The rug was custom made by Sacco Carpets NY.

Previous: The terrace cantilevers over the inn's sprawling lawn. On the other side of the tree line is Penobscot Bay and its rocky isles.

Above: The Shōwa-era screen depicting a pastoral scene has come to symbolize the peaceful life Will and Brett enjoy at their castle.

carvings of fantastical winged creatures, that one laid with fireclay tile in blue, yellow, green, and red. Less sexy was the kitchen, which they inherited out of code. Even worse than that was the cold snap that left Norumbega with a handful of burst pipes (luckily, the water damage was contained to the back of the house).

When it came time to decorate, Brett and Will were equally integral. In fact, Brett surprised everyone—even himself—by putting together a complete design deck. "It was the first and last deck I ever made," he says proudly. It was all Ralph Lauren furniture, fabric upon fabric, and "probably a little overboard in the chintz department." There was also no mention of budget, which, by and large, fell to Will. With the help of New York City interiors firm studiocake, they landed on a design directive that balanced everything: historical detail with contemporary design, castle-like grandeur with authentic Mainer style, and Brett's pie-in-the-sky vision with Will's disciplined architect's outlook.

Nearly every room was named for a European estate. Sandringham was wrapped in Schumacher green-and-white checkered wallpaper and filled with Victoriana nods both subtle and overt: a green canopy bed, a pair of nineteenth-century French Louis XIII–style armchairs with Aubusson tapestry upholstery. In Warwick, an original clawfoot tub and red-tiled fireplace were paired with velvet armchairs, a tufted mohair Regency bench, and "the Blue Lady," a painted portrait the couple found at Camden's Antiques at 10 Mechanic.

The three rooms in the attic—which Stearns was known to occupy on rainy nights, falling asleep to the music of the raindrops—were combined to create the Penthouse, and filled with uncommon finds like a pair of 1950s William Hinn lounge chairs, an antique inlaid wood escritoire, and a faux malachite-topped side table. The Library Suite is another ode to Norumbega's creator, built inside his duplex library, with a mezzanine lined with thousands of books, including an impressive collection of colorful *Reader's Digests*.

As it all came together, Brett became more and more connected to the inn. A year in, he began working with a local Camden voice coach—a music director for Carnegie Hall—and his visits to the city became less frequent. "I kept finding that every time I went back to the apartment, I would want to be in Maine," he says. (The couple sold their apartment shortly after reopening the inn on Memorial Day 2023.) Brett also found a passion for the theater of hospitality. He welcomes his guests with a warm sense of performance and keeps his set always opening-day-ready, curating playlists and swanning (always swanning) about, rotating this book just so and moving that vase of flowers to the other side of the room. "He's so good at giving hospitality," says Will, whose own days are filled with making repairs, balancing the ledger, managing contractors, and generally keeping the inner workings of a 140-year-old house in tip-top shape.

However unrealistic Brett's original design deck may have been, there is one piece—a splurge for sure—that made the final cut: an antique Shōwa-era screen depicting a pastoral scene of flowers, a bonsai tree, and two roosters. "I chased this piece for months and months, I wanted it so badly," recalls Brett. Only later, after it was hanging above the striped banquette in the dining room, did he realize what an unusual piece it was. "Normally in screens like this, when you see two roosters, they're fighting over territory, but in this depiction they are peaceful."

It's fitting, he says thoughtfully, "because what we love most about this place is working together and spending time together." Will and Brett—two peaceful kings in their castle.

Opposite: In the dining room, a velvet Arc sofa by TRNK and chartreuse Murano chandelier complement the blue tiles around the giant fireplace. The stained oak paneling throughout the ground floor was in exceptional shape.

Above: The sunlit room off the parlor is home to a vintage Yamaha baby grand piano that the couple purchased in Portland. The wood is a near-match for The Norumbega's elaborate oak paneling.

Clockwise from above:
The Norumbega was modeled after the great castles of Europe; the bar, painted a royal blue hue appropriately called Kensington, is a moody antechamber off the main dining room; a golden marker noting the date of construction, 1896, at the base of the castle's turret.

Clockwise from top left: Breakfast on the terrace; the vintage mismatched rug runners were an idea borrowed from one of Brett's design idols, Kelly Wearstler; in the bar, the pendant light with hand-blown glass globes is by Vitra while the gilt chandelier is from Gaetano Sciolari For Palwa.

Opposite: In the Library Suite, housed within the castle's original duplex library, a mezzanine lined with hundreds of books on mahogany shelves hovers over the bed.

Above: In the Sandringham Suite, a sitting area includes a pair of nineteenth-century French Louis XIII–style walnut chairs with Aubusson upholstering. Gambit wallpaper in sage from Schumacher sets the color palette for the suite.

Opposite and above: Kensington's yellow-tiled fireplace inspired an elegantly understated aesthetic, which includes Elizabeth Eakins Alur Green wallpaper, vintage brass candlesticks, and midcentury armchairs from 1stDibs.

The Party

Starts Here

THE VIEWPOINT

York, Maine

Joe Lipton has always been the good-time guy. Everybody knows one—the friend that doesn't just throw the party, he *is* the party. "Actually," he says with a grin, his eyes shaded by dark sunglasses, a Manhattan in his hand, "I hosted my high school graduation party—and I didn't even graduate." He's all energy. Pure, suntanned, ponytailed energy.

Good times aside, history shows that guys like Joe don't often win in life—and, early on, it seemed fairly evident to him that there wasn't much waiting for him on the proverbial career path. His childhood in the coastal town of York, Maine, had been loving, if unstable, and growing up in a single-parent household had left him aimless, rebellious. School wasn't for him, so he dropped out and took up construction. To satisfy his good-time-guy persona, he gigged as a DJ on weekends. Beyond that, there was no plan.

Which makes what happened next all the more incredible.

Joe found he was quite good at construction and, over time, jobs multiplied until he had become the go-to Mr. Fix-It for Chris Crane, an entrepreneur who had made his fortune investing in software businesses. Though Chris initially hired Joe to paint his house, he quickly saw potential in the young handyman, and over time, the businessman threw bigger and more complicated tasks at his charge. Chris would buy a new building; Joe would oversee the mechanics of it. Chris would buy a new company; Joe would manage the turnover. One by one, Joe would master each new challenge to

Joe Lipton & Michelle Friar

Page 272: The Shoreside rooms were carved into the property's grassy knoll, with concrete poured into board molds to capture the texture and grain of wood.

Previous: The Viewpoint, seen from Cape Neddick.

Above: The Airstream restaurant A Little Auk was one of Joe's many middle-of-the-night epiphanies, an answer to the pandemic-era's need for alfresco dining.

and the two had visited Oscar Niemeyer's French Communist Party headquarters, an elegant, curved concrete structure that had remained vivid in Joe's memory. "What if we built something *inside* the hill?" he asked Michelle, still half-asleep.

Board-formed concrete was the answer, inserted into the ground like a bunker, and, on the shoreside, a wall of windows. On the roof, grass was replanted to absorb rainwater and provide energy-efficient insulation. Inside, Michelle blended natural details with hints of 1950s nostalgia—midcentury modern chairs, blob mirrors, oak case goods—to pay homage to the site's first inn. More glass walls were installed in the interiors to ensure every nook would have a view: brush your teeth, shower, sleep, work—the Nubble lighthouse moves with you through the room. When the Shoreside Rooms at last opened, they were a hit. Joe and Michelle had made the most dramatic hotel rooms York had ever seen.

More brilliant ideas came, some by dream, others by chance. An Airstream-turned-bar was the basis for an alfresco restaurant called A Little Auk—another one of Joe's middle-of-the-night epiphanies—and behind that, a spa house for massages and facials. Down the road, the retro Nevada motel on Long Sands Beach hit the market, and Joe, Michelle, and Chris snapped that up and renovated it too. There, the family opened Lulu's, a tiki bar run by daughter Lydia and her chef husband.

By all accounts, Joe is the boss now. And often, he acts it. He quotes Maya Angelou to his staff and urges them to read his favorite book, Will Guidara's *Unreasonable Hospitality*. He has learned to trust his business instincts as he manages a team of more than one hundred. Still, you may be able to take Joe out of a party, but you can never take the party out of Joe. Several nights a week you'll find him and Michelle holding court over the Auk, Lulu's, or Stones Throw. Guests pour in to give the couple a hug or kiss and compliments on the lobster sliders and spicy margaritas. With their hospitality empire, they've created a warm welcome to those visiting their beloved hometown, as well as a pilgrimage of sorts for locals, who flow from one spot to the next for cocktails, dinner, and the kind of revelry only Joe can provide.

That it all stems from a chance encounter with Chris—now a father figure as much as a friend and business partner—is not lost on Joe. In fact, it seems to be his raison d'être. "Twenty years ago, I would have thought none of this could be possible," he says. "Until Chris, no one in my life ever told me that I could do big things." No longer the lost son wandering through life without guidance or goals, Joe has not one, but many families, in Michelle and his kids, in Chris, and in his ever-growing team. It's a much bigger party these days, but one thing's for sure: Joe is still the life of it.

Opposite: Michelle blended natural details with hints of 1950s nostalgia—midcentury modern furniture, oak case goods—to pay homage to York's first inn.

Above: Glass walls and floor-to-ceiling windows make sure the Nubble lighthouse is always in sight—even when you brush your teeth.

Above left and right, and opposite: Joe and Michelle insist that every day at The Viewpoint should be a party, with cocktails on the lawn, bottles of rosé in the rooms, and pizza and beer at A Little Auk.

Frizzante Rosé
THE VIEWPOINT HOTEL

Opposite: The Nubble lighthouse stands tall just across the cape from The Viewpoint's sprawling gardens.

Above left: The inn's cluster of clapboard cottages, framed by blooming hydrangea, climb a grassy hill overlooking the cape.

Above right: Joe and Michelle hold court at A Little Auk. The couple's York restaurants have become a nightly pilgrimage for many locals.

Acknowledgments

I'm told it is good form (and probably good luck) to thank your editor first, and I feel compelled to do so for more than propriety's sake. Thank you to Jenny Florence for believing in this project from day one, for greenlighting it within weeks (maternity leave pending!), and for being such a thoughtful, collaborative, and, frankly, gentle guide in the process of making my first book.

Thank you, beyond words, to the amazing people who make up *The Inn Crowd*. I really love you all and feel ridiculously honored that you have allowed me to photograph your beautiful spaces and share your inspiring stories. The fact that you all housed and fed me along the way is only further testament to your generosity—the very stuff of *The Inn Crowd* indeed! Most of all, I am thankful to you for so openly and honestly sharing your dreams with me; in turn, it allowed me to achieve my own dream with this book, and for that I am forever grateful.

Special thanks to Amanda and Joe at The Villa at Saugerties for being *The Inn Crowd*'s guinea pigs. Long before any book deal or publisher, you allowed me to barge into your lives with my incessant nudging of furniture and endless line of questioning. And sincere thanks to Bobbi Brown and Steven Plofker for writing the foreword of this book. Bobbi, you are an inspiration and role model in all that you have done. We all want to grow up to be like Bobbi!

More thanks to those who nudged this project along: To Leanne Drago, for being my chauffeur, my pro bono publicist, and the most enthusiastic cheerleader a girl could ask for. To Maura Egan and Alexander Galan for being the connectors that got my proposal into the right hands. To Gina Hamadey for opening the all-too-often-locked gate by sharing her own successful proposals. And to Jill Newman for being a sounding board every step of the way.

Thank you especially to Cantina's James Brown and Ana Rita Teodoro for making logical sense of my hundreds (thousands?) of photos, and for breathing colorful life into every chapter. Thank you also to Monacelli—the magical machine that made this happen—especially Michael Vagnetti and Laura Mintz, and to Kate Greenberg of Arply.

Lastly—but, really, firstly—thank you to John. For your patience and guidance, for lending your impeccable architect's eye on so many shoots, and for insisting that I always, *always* advocate for myself. You're still the best decision I ever made. I don't know who, what, or where I would be without you.

Directory

Tristate

LOST FOX INN
571 Torrington Road, Litchfield, CT 06759
(860) 222-0855
lostfoxinn.com

THE GEORGE
37 North Mountain Avenue, Montclair, NJ 07042
(973) 783-7878
thegeorgemontclair.com

GLENMERE MANSION
634 Pine Hill Road, Chester, NY 10918
(845) 469-1900
glenmeremansion.com

Long Island

THE ROUNDTREE, AMAGANSETT
273 Main Street, Amagansett, NY 11930
(631) 267-3133
theroundtreehotels.com

SILVER SANDS MOTEL & BEACH BUNGALOWS
1400 Silvermere Road, Greenport, NY 11944
(631) 997-1957
silversandsmotel.com

Upstate

EASTWIND HOTELS
eastwindhotels.com

Eastwind Oliverea Valley
212-220 Mckenley Hollow Road, Big Indian, NY 12410
(973) 566-4424

Eastwind Lake Placid
6048 Sentinel Road, Lake Placid, NY 12946
(518) 837-1882

Eastwind Windham
5088 Route 23, Windham, NY 12496
(518) 734-0553

INNS OF AURORA
378 Main Street, Aurora, NY 13026
(315) 364-8888
innsofaurora.com

THE VILLA AT SAUGERTIES
159 Fawn Road, Saugerties, NY 12477
(845) 246-5440
thevillaatsaugerties.com

THE HENSON
39 Goshen Road, Hensonville, NY 12439
(518) 734-4160
thehenson.com

FOSTER SUPPLY HOSPITALITY
fostersupplyco.com

Kenoza Hall
5762 NY State Route 52, Kenoza Lake, NY
(845) 482-1022
kenozahall.com

The Arnold House
839 Shandelee Road, Livingston Manor, NY 12758
(845) 439-5070
thearnoldhouse.com

Hemlock Neversink
7491 State Route 55, Neversink, NY 12765
(845) 985-1183
hemlockneversink.com

The DeBruce
982 Debruce Road, Livingston Manor, NY 12758
(845) 439-3900
thedebruce.com

The Berkshires

THE INN AT KENMORE HALL
1385 State Road, Richmond, MA 01254
(413) 698-8100
theinnatkenmorehall.com

GRANVILLE HOUSE
98 Division Street, Great Barrington, MA, 01230
(201) 450-1824
granvillehouseinn.com

Vermont

THE INN AT BURKLYN
2864 Darling Hill Road, East Burke, VT 05832
(802) 626-1111
theinnatburklyn.com

EDSON HILL
1500 Edson Hill Road, Stowe, VT 05672
(802) 253-7371
edsonhill.com

Maine

THE NORUMBEGA INN
63 High Street, Camden, ME 04843
(207) 236-4646
norumbegainn.com

THE VIEWPOINT
229 Nubble Road, York, ME 03909
(207) 361-3261
viewpointhotel.com

Monacelli
A Phaidon Company
111 Broadway
New York, NY 10006

Phaidon Press Limited
2 Cooperage Yard
London E15 2QR

Phaidon SARL
55, rue Traversière
75012 Paris

phaidon.com/monacelli

First published 2025

ISBN 978-1-58093-696-5

Library of Congress Control Number: 2025934606

Editor: Jenny Florence
Production Director: Michael Vagnetti
Design: Ana Rita Teodoro, Cantina
Printed in China